COOK'S ARK

The animals that sailed with James Cook

First published 2019

ISBN 978-0-473-49316-5

A catalogue record for this book is available from the National Library of New Zealand

Maps 1, 3-6: Natalie Douglas, Crave Design Ltd, NZ

Map 2: Roger Smith, Geographx Ltd, Wellington

Cover & contents page images: Alan Sanders, NZ Marine & Portrait Artist.

Cover, interior design and typesetting: Rachel Stevens

Printed in New Zealand by Your Books, Wellington

COOK'S ARK

The animals that sailed with James Cook

ALISON SUTHERLAND

*For the Arapawa Goat family,
you are as unique as the animals you are trying to save.*

CONTENTS

Acknowledgements

At some point along the journey of gathering material for *Cook's Ark*, I stopped writing to inform and allowed the story to take on a life of its own. This new pathway led me towards the most amazing people, all of them experts and passionate about different aspects that, when woven together, brought life and substance into what was originally just a framework of historical data. As the manuscript grew, so too did the list of people I must acknowledge for their input. In no particular order of contribution or importance, I publically thank the following, and apologise profusely to those I may have inadvertently overlooked.

To New Zealand's National Library, you are such a treasure trove, a Taonga freely available for all to explore New Zealand's history. More locally, I thank the wonderful staff at the Masterton Library. To New Zealand's Art Gallery, the Australian Maritime Museum and to the lovely ladies at the Mitchell Library in Sydney, the British Library for the generous permissions and the British Museum for responding so promptly to my queries and walking me through their processes.

Special thanks to Alan Sanders, for capturing the substance of what I was trying to convey in his paintings. These will forever symbolise for me *Cook's Ark*. For the information regarding early navy terminology and procedures, I am beholden to John Allan, an ex-Naval man and academic who spent decades studying Cook's voyages and the ships he sailed in. It was John's suggestion of an animal connection to his ship that started me on the search for *Resolution's* figurehead. Thank you, John, for your priceless advice on all things nautical, for your meticulous editing of the early manuscript, and for the rich and invigorating discussions around Captain Cook's journeys. So often, a writer works through paper or screen. To sit down at a table with someone and be encouraged to talk about one's passion is such a wonderful gift. Special thanks too, to John Robson, a scholar and the President of the Captain Cook Society. His book, *Captain Cook's World*, was the go-to text when checking locations and dates throughout Cook's voyages. Because *Cook's Ark* is non-fiction, the historical accuracy provided by John of Cook's route and ports of call were essential.

I am indebted to the Captain Cook Society, both the UK and the NZ branches, for all their support and information. Also to Michaela King for permission to include the image of her late father's etching. Thanks also to John Palmer for his enthusiasm and expertise on historical poultry breeds, and for sharing so much so freely. Lex McKay for creating some colourful sketches and the excitement that these evoked as the story unfolded. Lex, your passion and positivity gave me the energy that was needed to bring *Cook's Ark* to the stage where, at last, I could put down the pen.

To Alan. For fifty years, you have been the wind beneath my wings. Thank you for the endless coffees, for never complaining when the research and manuscript became my entire focus, and for putting up with the glow in the night as I once again put pen to paper. Thank you for patiently listening to every theory and every sentence, and for accommodating my need to read out loud what I had written. Who knew you could be so tolerant.

When I commenced this journey, because that is what it is to write a book such as this, I had hoped to find answers to the mystery that surrounds the origins of New Zealand's beautiful and precious Arapawa goats. The historical evidence pointed us in several directions. It was the wonderful work of three amazing scientists: Doctors McEwan, Lanstra and Sponenberg, that now enable us to bury the urban myth and celebrate the real story of New Zealand's unique heritage goat. On behalf of the Arapawa goat family, we thank you. To those people who have been disappointed by the findings of my research into the origins of the Arapawa goats, please be comforted in the knowledge that while it is the end of a popular legend, it is the beginning of a new story for these critically endangered animals. Their true story, supported by scientific and historical evidence rather than myth, offers them a greater chance of survival.

Alison

PREFACE

Cook's Ark began with goats. A popular New Zealand urban legend of the twentieth century was that English goats, secreted onto Arapawa Island's East Bay during Captain James Cook's second voyage, were the final remnants of a breed — the Old English goat — that became extinct in the 1950s. In response to the New Zealand Department of Conservation's eradication programme on Arapawa (now Arapaoa) Island, I established the New Zealand Arapawa Goat Association (NZAGA). The goal was to develop a breeding programme for the goats off the island to ensure the survival of their genetic diversity. Having a background in research (PhD in Education, Victoria University of Wellington, 2006), I began studying the history of the goats, reading old manuscripts, including the journals of James Cook. The stories that unfolded were so different from the history taught at school. Inspired by the delightful story of a ten-year-old Māori boy and an Old English goat, I wrote and published a children's illustrated book, *Old Will,* in 2013. A copy of this book was donated to every primary school, intermediate and public library throughout New Zealand. As the research continued, so too did my knowledge. A second book, *No Ordinary Goat,* written for adults, was published in 2016.

My enthusiasm for the Arapawa goats soon encompassed other livestock breeds introduced during the period of Cook's voyages, not only in New Zealand, but across the South Pacific. The more I read, the more fascinated I became by the stories of animals on Cook's voyages. Who knew seamen took pets on board sailing ships, that Cook's life was once saved by a dog, and sea-hardened sailors cried at the death of a little bird? The manuscripts revealed images of a hundred men and hundreds of animals squashed together on a ship not much larger than the average house. The hardships they suffered, their day-to-day existence — these stories brought the voyages of Cook alive for me; from these, *Cook's Ark* was born.

This book is more than just the retelling of old stories. Based on nine years of research, it is a collection of events involving animals during Cook's three voyages to the South Pacific. Within the stories is evidence of a relatively recent occurrence of animal population drift. This was the start of an evolutionary period for the South Pacific, where new species and breeds, introduced and, in some cases, released into the wild to survive, adapted to the ecological environment and evolved into something unique and special.

Nothing has been omitted that might offend or disturb, either because of the brutal details that occurred during such sea voyages, or because it does not conveniently adhere to current acceptance of behaviour or facts surrounding Cook's voyages.

To appreciate how an animal species or breed, previously unknown to Māori, Australian Aboriginals and Polynesians, arrived in the South Pacific, it has been necessary to provide some historical framework. To ensure the focus remains on the animals, a considerable amount of historical background relevant to James Cook's voyages is omitted. Where the reader wishes to gain a broader understanding of the history during the period of Cook's voyages, I strongly recommend J.C. Beaglehole's *The Journals of Captain James Cook on his Voyages of Discovery* and, to greater appreciate the Māori perspective, Dame Anne Salmond's *Two Worlds*, as well as *Between Worlds* and *The Trial of the Cannibal Dog*. For details around Cook's exploration of Australia, I recommend the work of Rob Mundle, a master of Australia's maritime history. For the islands of Polynesia, *Tupaia* by Joan Druett is a 'must-read'. There are occasions in the narrative where the European explorers' imperialistic viewpoints of that day are evident. These are clearly ignorant, prejudicial and offensive; therefore, while maintaining the text in quotations, I have used more respectful modern terms throughout my own narrative.

The London Gazette

EXTRAORDINARY.

No. 7   **SATURDAY 3 SEPTEMBER 1768**   TWO PENCE

Ladies & Gentlemen. We are in an exciting age of exploration. Britain has mastered the Oceans and is now reaching for the Sky. The Royal Society will attempt to calculate the distance of the Earth from the Sun. Following the suggestion made by Edmund Halley in 1716, Navy ships will carry astronomers to various locations around the world. Each will measure how long it takes Venus to cross the face of the sun. One of the chosen locations is to be a recently discovered island in the South Pacific. If we miss this opportunity, the next transit of Venus will not occur for over one hundred years. Let us hope for clear skies on 3 June, 1769. Read the headlines below to see how the story has unfolded.

The Scots Magazine

January 1768:510

To the author of the Scots Magazine.

Sir, Many attempts have been made to solve the ancient, curious, and difficult problem, viz. To find the sun's distance from the Earth. There was lately a meeting of astronomers at London to concert measures for observing the approaching transit of Venus over the sun's disk, in order therefrom to determine the sun's distance.

Oxford Journal

2 April 1768

Lieutenant Isieniel, an Officer in the Russian Service, set out last month from Petersburgh, with two officers and an escort, for Jakutz, in order to view at that place the Transit of Venus over the Sun.

The Manchester Mercury

Tuesday 31 May 1768. Numb. 887

By his Majesty's Ship *Dolphin*, newly arrived from a Voyage round the World, we hear, that they have discovered a new Island in the South Seas, large, fertile, and extremely populous. The *Dolphin* came to Anchor in a safe, spacious, and commodious Harbour, where she lay about six Weeks. From the behaviour of the Inhabitants, they had reason to believe she was the first and only Ship they had ever seen. ... We took Possession of the Island in his Majesty's Name, and called it King George's Land. It lies about 20 Degrees Southern Latitude.

SALISBURY AND WINCHESTER JOURNAL

25 July, 1768

Mr. John Gore, who served as Midshipman of the *Dolphin* man of war, under Commodore Byron, in her first voyage round the world, and as Mate and Pilot of that ship, under Captain Wallis in her second voyage, is promoted by the Lords of the Admiralty as third Lieutenant of the *Endeavour* Bark, Mr. James Cook, Lieutenant and Commander, bound to the South Sea, under the direction of the Royal Society. – Banks, Esq; a gentleman of considerable fortune, and several other gentlemen skilled in Astronomy, Botany, and Natural History, are going out in the said bark, which is fallen down to Blackwall, and is to sail in about a fortnight.

Oxford Journal

30 July, 1768

Mr Edward Webster, of St. Neot's in Huntingdonshire is solicited by the Royal Academy of Sciences at Leyden, to go to the City of Batavia, in the East Indies ... to be ready to go from that Place to one of the Islands in the Eastern Ocean, which he shall judge most proper, to observe the Transit of the Planet Venus over the Sun, which will happen June 3d, 1769.

Archer's Bath Chronicle

12 August 1768

This morning Mr. Banks, Dr. Solano, and Mr. Green, the astronomer, set out for Deal, to embark on board the *Endeavour*, Captain Cook, for the South Seas, under the direction of the royal society, to observe the transit of Venus next summer, and to make discoveries to the south and west of Cape Horn.

Bath Chronicle and Weekly Gazette

25 August 1768

The gentlemen, who are to sail in a few days for George's Land, the new discovered island in the Pacific ocean, with an intention to observe the Transit of Venus, are likewise, we are credibly informed, to attempt some new discoveries in that vast unknown tract, above the latitude 40.

We are confident that our readers will join with us in wishing all who sail on *Endeavour* a safe journey around the World. And let us not forget the little goat that will sail on her. The very same animal that has only just completed her first circumnavigation on *Dolphin,* is now sailing around the world for a second time.

PART ONE

Cook's First Voyage Around The World

Chapter 1

PREPARING TO SAIL

After months of preparation, Lieutenant James Cook was ready to embark on his greatest adventure: a voyage to the South Pacific Ocean. This was his first time sailing as a commander, although without the rank of Captain at this stage. His destination was to be King George's Island (Otaheite/Tahiti), an island newly found in the South Pacific by Samuel Wallis in *Dolphin*. The purpose of Cook's voyage, as instructed by the Admiralty, was to observe and record the transit of the planet Venus across the face of the sun.

His ship was *Endeavour*, a 106-foot long, three-masted, flat-bottomed coal ship previously named *Earl of Pembroke*. A man from the working classes and not yet forty, Cook was about to become the master of his own ship. He must have been excited at the prospect, yet when he arrived at the Royal Navy's Deptford dockyard, he maintained a facade of calmness and quiet authority.

THE MEN

When Cook approached his ship on 7 August 1768, most of the officers and crew were already on board *Endeavour*. Zachary Hicks, a Londoner, had been appointed his Second Lieutenant. He was unknowingly infected with tuberculosis. Cook's Third Lieutenant was John Gore, an American who had been Master's Mate on *Dolphin* under both John Byron and Samuel Wallis. Gore was an experienced mariner and would prove to be a huge asset to Cook as he knew more about the Pacific than any other man on *Endeavour*. Rising quickly through the ranks was Englishman and Master's Mate Charles Clerke. He too had earlier sailed on *Dolphin* and would go on to command the support ship on Cook's third voyage. He had a boisterous sense of humour and a generous spirit, and being a farmer's son, was well acquainted with animal husbandry.

Other men who transferred from *Dolphin* were Robert Molyneux, twenty-two years old (a man who liked his drink); teenager Richard Pickersgill, already an experienced seaman and an astronomer; and Welshman Francis Wilkinson. Two more key players on this voyage were William Monkhouse, the ship's surgeon, and his brother Jonathan Monkhouse, a midshipman. Rarely mentioned in the literature, but nevertheless playing an important role with the animals on *Endeavour*, were John Thompson, the one-handed ship's cook who was responsible for providing food for the crew; and Henry Jeffs, the ship's butcher.

Cook, satisfied that everything was secure, relocated *Endeavour* from Deptford to Plymouth. A complement of twelve marines, led by Sergeant John Edgcumbe, were there waiting to be received on board. Marines were necessary aboard sailing ships as they protected the ship from attack, against mutiny, kept watch over stores, especially food and water; and helped out on various non-nautical duties.

On Sunday, 14 August 1768, twenty-four-year-old Joseph Banks, wealthy socialite, naturalist and botanist, and a close friend of Lord Sandwich, the First Lord of the Admiralty, joined the expedition. Accompanying him were his Swedish colleagues, Dr Daniel Solander (a fellow naturalist and Banks's librarian) and Herman Spöring (Banks's secretary). The scientists would be travelling with them. Already on board were Banks's retinue of an astronomer, Charles Green; the artists Alexander Buchan and Sydney Parkinson; his assistants Peter Briscoe, James Roberts and John Reynolds; and two African servants, George Dorlton and Thomas Richmond.

Banks had been advised by his good friend Thomas Pennant, an esteemed naturalist, to take a water dog and a fleet dog with him. Tightly restrained by Dorlton and Richmond were a male greyhound[1] and a bitch by the name of 'Lady'.[2] As well as the men and dogs, Banks brought with him his personal supply of brandy, salted cabbage, sheep, chickens and pigs. With little available space on *Endeavour* to store all his stuff, Banks opted to sling a hammock in the Great Cabin for himself, while his dogs and their

attendants slept in the cramped adjoining cabin reserved for him. Aware that Banks had paid to enlarge the Great Cabin to cater for himself and his assistants, Cook did not protest. The inexperienced commander was yet to assert his authority over the arrogant young aristocrat who had paid a fortune to join the expedition.

Ninety-four men, together with supplies sufficient for an eighteen-month sea voyage, were packed on the shallow-bottomed bark built for a crew of twenty. A sailing ship was powered by the labour of its crew, and food fuelled the seamen. This is why *Endeavour* was overcrowded with men, dried provisions and livestock.

The Animals

While Cook was learning about the officers, crew and gentlemen who would sail with him, English livestock destined as fresh food — pigs, cattle, sheep and poultry — was being loaded on board *Endeavour*[3] No space had been specifically allocated for livestock below decks. To have defecating, urinating and farting animals in such proximity to men crammed together in a confined space would be unbearable. The animals, bleating, mooing and grunting in protest, instead went into purpose-built pens on the upper deck. Squawking poultry was packed tightly together in cages, which were stacked in the small boats or lashed to the railings. The decision to have all the livestock out in the open and vulnerable to the elements would have dire consequences.

Some animals were allowed below. As well as Banks's dogs, squeezed on board was a small milking goat who would supply fresh milk for the officers and gentlemen's coffee throughout the voyage. This extraordinary goat, said to be quite a 'sea dog' and a good milker, had only recently returned from circumnavigating the world with Samuel Wallis in *Dolphin*.[4] Also on *Endeavour* were three cats. While aboard primarily to control the disease-carrying rodent and insect population, they also served as pets for the men. Cats were also an effective warning system of approaching bad weather. When a healthy cat refused to leave its shelter, the old mariners knew to fasten the hatches. We now know that cats can sense barometric pressure changes.

Chapter 2

The First Voyage

England to South America

All was ready on *Endeavour*. And so they waited for the right winds to come. For days they waited, until at last, on 25 August 1768, the desired winds breathed into the sails. At 3 p.m. Cook gave the order to raise the anchors on his overladen ship. Accompanied by small boats and screeching seagulls, they sailed out of the English Channel into the Bay of Biscay, straight into a violent storm. As *Endeavour* bucked and rolled, huge waves crashed over the outer decks. Most of the poultry, their crates secured to the railings on the upper deck, drowned. This was a huge loss as they were there to provide eggs for the officers, the gentlemen and the sick, and once past their egg-laying days they would add fresh meat to the diet, and their feathers would be turned into quills for writing. Replacement poultry would have to be purchased at their first port of call, Madeira.

The remaining livestock, though saturated in their pens, survived the brutal squall. Joseph Banks's dogs, safely tucked up in their master's cabin, were fine. The ship's cats, always free to search for vermin, soon learnt where there were small spaces to keep them safe and dry. The goat, berthed in a dry, dark corner of the lower deck, passively waited for the milk to be stripped from her burgeoning udder. Experienced seafarers knew storms at sea had a positive side. Rainwater would replenish water stocks and dead animals meant additional meat for the soup. Nothing would be wasted – not the feathers, the meat, the hide, or any other part of a deceased animal. The only exceptions were animals that the superstitious seamen believed would bring them bad luck, ill health or death: sharks and albatrosses.

Cook's Orders to the Men

After the storm abated, Cook gathered all the people together to give them instructions for the voyage. He was convinced that fresh and pickled foods, good hygiene and rest were the keys to preventing disease on board ship. The men would eat the beef when served to them. When the fresh fruit, meat, vegetables and fish were exhausted, sauerkraut (made of fermented cabbage) would supplement the salted meat, pease soup and biscuits. The men shuffled their feet and moaned in protest. Cook quietened the disgruntled crew by telling them that combined with a change in their diet there would be a change in their conditions. He ordered three watches instead of the customary two, which gave them eight

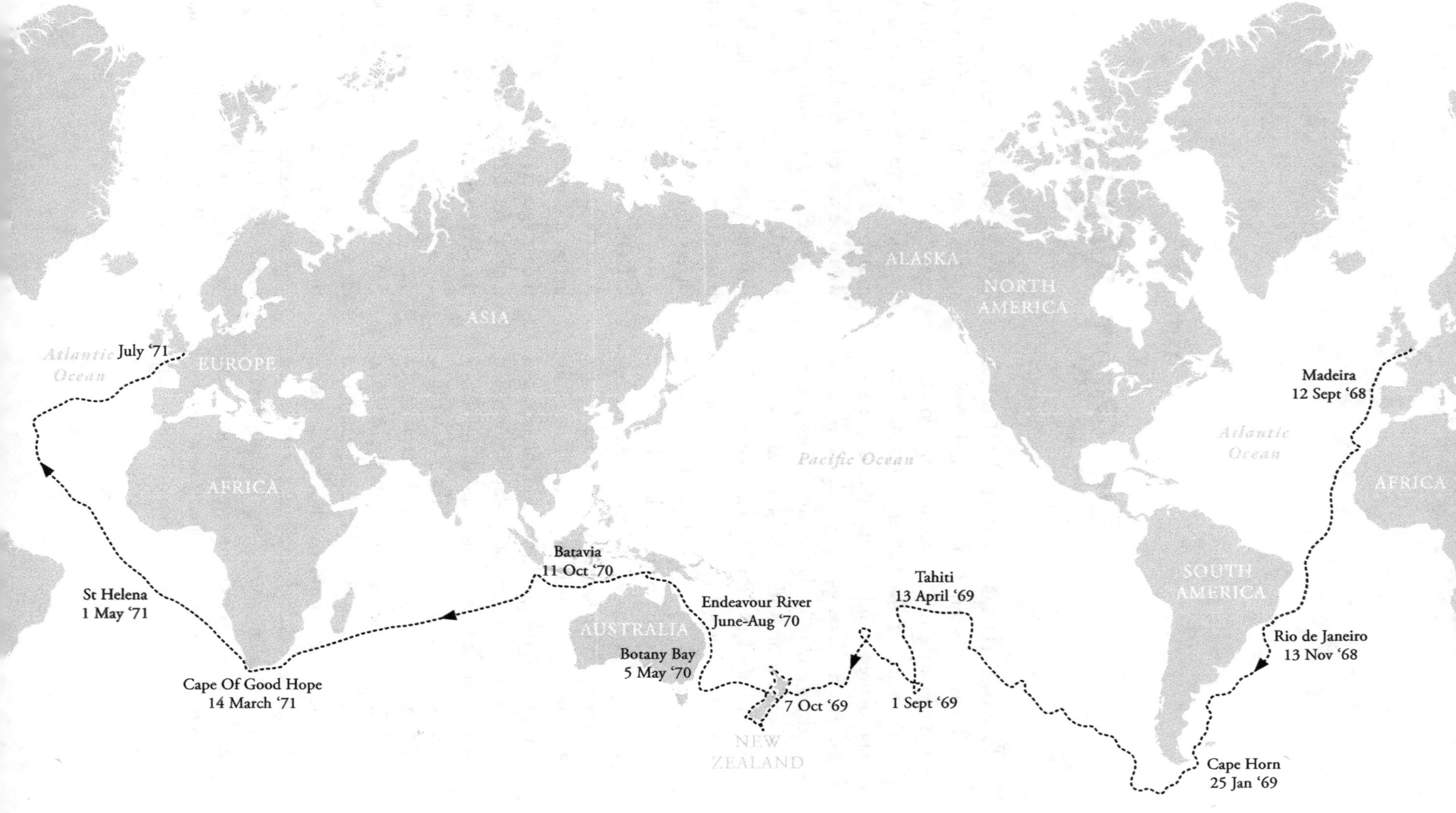

Cook's First Voyage in Endeavour
ASIA
ALASKA
NORTH AMERICA
EUROPE
AFRICA
SOUTH AMERICA
AFRICA
AUSTRALIA
NEW ZEALAND
Atlantic Ocean
Pacific Ocean
Atlantic Ocean
July '71
Madeira
12 Sept '68
St Helena
1 May '71
Cape Of Good Hope
14 March '71
Batavia
11 Oct '70
Endeavour River
June-Aug '70
Botany Bay
5 May '70
7 Oct '69
Tahiti
13 April '69
1 Sept '69
Rio de Janeiro
13 Nov '68
Cape Horn
25 Jan '69

hours off duty instead of the usual four. Cook was determined to run a humane and clean ship. The men were to change and clean their clothes on a regular basis. They would have at least one cold, saltwater bath a day when the weather was fair. The old custom of washing their clothes in urine was unacceptable. While the ammonia in the urine might act as a detergent, the smell below decks of over ninety men living together and wearing clothes washed in this way would be horrendous. They would air their hammocks, clothing and bedding outside every three days. Crew would scour the decks with salt water and vinegar. They were also rostered to control the vermin on board by scrubbing and fumigating between the decks with smoke generated from burning soiled hay and wood clippings. The seamen understood the necessity to control the rats, mice, fleas, flies and cockroaches as they carried disease, but it was the cockroaches and rats that they feared the most.

No one was exempt from these orders, including Banks and his entourage. Cook was beginning to assert his authority.

COCKROACHES

In the warm damp of the lower decks, amongst the decaying firewood, planks and timbers of sailing ships, cockroaches nested and lay their eggs. When they entered the warmer climates, the eggs would hatch and the ship would be overrun with the almost indestructible insects. Seamen were terrified of them. Cockroaches would drop down from the ceiling and land on the men as they slept in their hammocks, seeking a feast of dead tissue. Hard skin on the soles of the feet, fingernails, toenails, eyelashes, even bunions on the feet, were tasty morsels for these pests. Even worse was the fear a cockroach would burrow into a man's ears and lay its eggs.

Spiders and ants, however, were desirable passengers on sailing ships, as they attacked and fed on the young cockroaches.

SHIP'S RATS

Black rat, etching by W.S. Howitt, 1801 (Wikimedia commons).

While the cockroaches were feared, the ship's rats (the black rat) were the vermin the men hated the most. Rats had the potential to do the most damage during the voyage.[5] A combination of an unquenchable thirst and four front teeth that grew continuously unless checked by constant use made the rat the most formidable pest on any sailing ship. Rats, in their desperate search for water, gnawed under the waterways of the deck until it became so thin they could suck moisture through it. Wooden casks containing precious water, wine, rum and brandy were another target for thirsty rats. The barrels required a constant guard to ensure rats could not access them. Driven by their thirst, rats would nibble at exterior planks close to the seam until the seawater trickled through. If the holes the rats made were under the waterline in a concealed part of the ship they became life threatening. Having made holes and finding the salt water unpalatable, the rats would search for other sources of liquid. They would climb the shrouds that serve to hold up the masts, sucking water from the gaps amongst the rigging. When it rained, the rats would become so bold they would scamper around the decks, ignoring the seamen.

Cook's orders to fumigate the ship would only be a temporary measure to rid *Endeavour* of rats. As soon as they neared the shore, rats would swim to the ship in swarms, crawl up the cables and find places to hide and feast. Putting a circular piece of wood around the cables to stop rats climbing on board sometimes worked, but loading stores onto a ship would also attract the rodents.

While rats put the ship in constant danger, they also had their uses. When all the livestock were gone, other than the ship's cats and the men's pets, the rats were their only source of fresh meat.

The Swedish botanist Anders Sparrman, one of the observers on Cook's second voyage, shared a tale about two Englishmen on *Resolution*, a midshipman and an aged quartermaster, who developed a taste for rat meat. The midshipman had a favourite cat who would catch a rat and bring it back to him to cut it up. He would divide her prey so that she got the fore part 'and the back part was cleaned, roasted, and peppered for himself.'[6] Sparrman said the two men would enjoy their fresh food while others moaned about their daily diet of biscuit and the rationed salted meat.

First Destination, Madeira

Endeavour's first destination was Madeira, off north-west Africa, to pick up fresh supplies. As they sailed south two birds flew into the rigging, evidently blown from land, became entangled, and their dead bodies discarded overboard. As they were of an

Cat, Bewick: 205

unknown species, Banks expressed a desire to examine a live one. An enterprising young man caught one, a wagtail, the following day and took it to Banks who named the species *Motacilla velificans*. The exhausted bird died within minutes of being handed to Banks.

They reached Madeira on 12 September where, only two weeks out from England, they lost their first man. The quartermaster, Scotsman Alexander Weir, had his leg entangled in a buoy rope while he was retrieving an anchor. The weight of the anchor dragged him overboard, and by the time they retrieved him he had drowned. There was little time to mourn a man they barely knew.

Banks and Solander went off on a botanical mission, and while they were gone fruit, onions, fresh beef, pork and mutton, along with casks of rum and fine wine, were loaded on board *Endeavour*. At Madeira they were able to purchase more chickens to replace those they had lost in the storm. They also bought a bullock for future slaughter.[7] The men collected fresh, clean hay for the animals and stored it under cover in the small boats on the upper deck. Stuffed into any available space on the decks below was surplus hay that would not fit in the boats.

Conscious of changing weather patterns, Cook decided it was time to move on. They left Madeira at midnight on 18 September, sailing with the Atlantic Ocean's north-east trade winds.

MADEIRA TO SOUTH AMERICA

The weather pleasant and the sea calm, the men would entertain themselves on the outside deck, fishing, catching birds, sometimes whittling wood or just sunbathing. Mingling amongst them enjoying the sun

would be the nanny goat. Exercised under the watchful eye of crew on duty would be pigs, sheep and the odd cattle beast. Henry Jeffs, the butcher, would likely be busy slaughtering some animal, no doubt closely watched by Banks's dogs and the ship's cats.

Observed following *Endeavour* on 29 September was a young shark. A line was put out, the shark took the bait and it was hauled on board, bringing with it four sucking fish. The scientists thoroughly enjoyed the stew made from the shark, but the crew would not eat it. Banks scoffed at the seamen's unwillingness to eat a species that fed on human flesh. Later that evening a swallow and two wagtails began fluttering around the ship. A man caught the wagtail and delivered it to Banks. While examining the small bird, Banks noted some subtle differences between

The 'Great Cabin' referred to by Banks, as shown on the replica 'HMB Endeavour' berthed at Darling Harbour, Sydney, 25 November 2018. At the top right is a reproduction of the 'brace/cage' used by Banks to contain the captured bird. The opening at the back of the Great Cabin leads into Banks' small berth where his dogs lived during the voyage. (Author's photo).

the earlier wagtail and this one, so he labelled it *Motacilla avida*. Forming an attachment to the bird and hoping to keep it alive, Banks had a brace (metal cage) made by the ship's ironmonger. Every living thing on board had its place. Flies abounded on board *Endeavour*, so Banks hung the cage from a beam in the Great Cabin and the bird was free to fly around in search of its own dinner.

The Great Cabin, situated at the rear of the ship, had large windows to let in natural light and quickly became the naturalists' domain. The artists, Buchan and Parkinson, sketched in one space, while Banks and Solander dissected and examined specimens on the main table, with Spöring taking notes as they worked. On the same table, Cook spread out his charts, recorded events and tried to focus on the journey ahead. Cook sometimes left the larger room to work in his tiny cabin, the ceiling so low he had to bend in half to enter the doorway. Cook's cabin became his refuge. It was quieter than the Great Cabin, which not only contained the scientists with their assistants and servants coming and going, but also Banks' dogs, the occasional cat searching for vermin, and now a bird flying around after flies, no doubt leaving its droppings around the place.

The wagtail survived for over three weeks until one of the ship's cats finally caught it. Banks, who daily dissected and preserved animal specimens, mourned the death of his feathered pet and was moved to write in his diary: 'Today the cat killd our bird M. Avida who had lived with us ever since the 29th of September entirely on the flies which he caught for himself; he was hearty and in high health so that probably he might have lived a great while longer had fate been more kind.'[8]

Endeavour crossed the equator on 25 October 1768. Tradition had it that those who had crossed the equator previously could claim the right to initiate those who had not done so. This was an accepted rite of passage from landlubber to seafarer. As Lieutenant John Gore was the highest-ranked officer who had crossed the line (while serving with Wallis on *Dolphin*), he was granted the privilege of calling everyone onto the quarterdeck (the raised deck behind the main mast) to be examined. Those who had never crossed the equator had their names added to a blacklist. Unless they paid the agreed fine of four days' allowance of brandy, rum or wine, those on the blacklist would be tied to a chair and plunged into the ocean three times. No person or pet was exempt. Excluded were the livestock, as they were on board as food, not seafarers. Added to the list were Banks's dogs, the ship's cats, James Cook, Doctor Solander and Joseph Banks. To avoid the ordeal, Banks paid the forfeit for himself, his assistants and servants. Disinclined to see them suffer, Banks also paid the tariff for his attendants and his two fortunate dogs.[9] Banks had little empathy for the ship's cats, so it is unlikely he paid their tariff. Perhaps some of the crew paid their ransom or, given they were such a necessity on board ship, their dunking was only a token gesture. The small milking goat was safe, as she had earlier crossed the line on *Dolphin*.

The heat and humidity increased as they sailed through the tropics on a westerly course. Items made of metal began to rust and possessions made of leather or paper became slimy with mildew. It had been over seven weeks since they left Madeira. With most of the livestock and other fresh provisions gone, everyone was looking forward to reaching the friendly port of Rio de Janeiro.

UNWELCOME AT RIO DE JANEIRO

Anchoring in Rio de Janeiro's harbour on Sunday, 13 November, nearly two months after they left Madeira, Cook's expectations of a friendly welcome were rudely dashed. The Portuguese Viceroy was ignorant of the transit of Venus, and suspicious of the Englishmen's intent. A collier, *Endeavour* did not look like a ship belonging to the Royal Navy. Suspecting they might be smugglers, or even spies, the nervous viceroy refused to allow the majority of the men ashore. Requests by Cook to allow the animals to graze on land were also denied. Frustrated, Cook stressed that his men and the animals were ill and starving. The viceroy allowed the surgeon to go on shore and Cook could buy provisions, but he would have to work through an agent.

For three weeks the ship's surviving livestock remained penned on the upper deck, their only relief being short walks on the deck under the careful watch of junior seamen. Being tame, Banks's dogs, the ship's cats and the nanny goat were free to roam around the ship.

Confined to *Endeavour*, bored and keen to collect unfamiliar plants and insect specimens, the naturalists resorted to scavenging through greens brought on board for the livestock. Irritated at the restrictions, Banks and Solander made plans to leave the ship so they could explore and gather samples outside the town boundary. To avoid being caught by the viceroy's guard,

they waited until a passing squall of wind and rain gave them cover, then at midnight they squeezed out of the cabin window, let themselves down into a boat conveniently tied close by, and slipped away with the tide. Once they were out of hearing, they rowed to an unfrequented part of the shore, where they landed and made for the countryside in search of botanical treasures.

Returning Banks and Solander to *Endeavour* without detection required a clever plan. The squall developed into a storm and after it had eased, Cook reported to the viceroy that two of *Endeavour*'s boats, the longboat and the yawl (a small boat), had broken their mooring lines. With the viceroy's permission, Cook sent men out in search of the lost vessels and, fortuitously, both boats were found undamaged and all his men, including the two scientific gentlemen, no doubt with smiles on their faces, were accounted for. Several days after this event, the viceroy gave permission for Cook's men to go ashore so *Endeavour* could be prepared for sail. A delighted Banks spent days wandering the countryside and collecting new specimens.

On 1 December Cook declared *Endeavour* suitably prepared for the next part of the voyage. With their casks now full of water, they took on board fresh supplies, including rum, fruit, vegetables, more pigs and some Muscovy ducks. As they prepared to sail out of the harbour, they lost their next man. Eighteen-year-old able seaman Peter Flower fell from the main shrouds into the sea and drowned. Flower had earlier served with Cook for five years on the Newfoundland survey ship, *Grenville*. Loyal to Cook, he had opted to go with him to the South

Pacific, along with four other men from the *Grenville*: Thomas Hardman, Isaac Smith, William Howson and John Charlton.[10] Even though Cook knew Death was an uninvited passenger on all long sea voyages, Flower's demise must have deeply affected him. However, Cook was a professional seaman so he hired a Portuguese sailor to replace Flower, and without any display of emotion, recorded the passing of his young friend. The men acknowledged the loss of Flower, then continued the tasks that would take *Endeavour* out of the safe harbour and towards the notorious Cape Horn.

Sailing towards Cape Horn

After leaving Rio de Janeiro, they continued south along the coast of Brazil with the goal of rounding Cape Horn and entering the South Pacific Ocean. Over the next few weeks the temperature steadily dropped and icy gales lashed the small ship. They were tormented by huge swells, hail and lightning. Exposed to the elements, freezing animals cowered together in their stalls on the upper deck. For days *Endeavour* pitched and rolled while the exhausted crew struggled to keep her afloat. When the sea calmed, the larger animals were taken out of their pens and exercised along the deck. The poultry and smaller animals remained in their enclosures while their soiled hay was removed and replaced. With nothing wasted on this long, arduous voyage, the used hay, with faeces and urine washed off with salt water, was fed to the starving, rapidly diminishing livestock. Sailing to the south, nearer to the freezing Antarctic Circle, men were engaged in repairing and preparing sails, while others made thick woollen clothing, particularly Fearnought (Magellan) jackets and trousers of heavy woollen cloth.

On Christmas Day 1768 the sea was calm and the men, as was the tradition on sailing ships, got abominably drunk. Four days later, closer to the coast, they sailed into debris of reeds, feathers and drowned beetles that Banks recorded as 'Carabi' and was probably a species of aquatic beetle in the family Carabidae.[11] Banks was quick to gather up some samples but was even more delighted the next day when huge quantities of seabirds and winged beetles flew around the ship. Banks's pleasure was short-lived when the beetles swarmed the deck. He swept some up and found they were full of tiny mites. As the day darkened, thunder roared and lightning, sometimes horizontal, sometimes vertical, streaked across the sky. The lightning gave Banks just enough light to see what appeared to be a red whale with a black tail; it was covered in barnacles. The squall passed and was followed by calm. So near land, insects blown out to sea would float past. Banks leaned over the railings for hours, fishing them up with a net, while offering volunteers a bottle of rum if they would help him.

They sighted Tierra del Fuego on 11 January 1769.

Tragedy at Tierra del Fuego

At daybreak on 15 January, *Endeavour* anchored in one of Tierra del Fuego's small bays that Cook would document as the 'Bay of Good Success'. Today it is known as Bahía Buen Suceso. Scattered around the bay were herds of seals and sea lions. Inland they met with a group of about sixty dark-haired people who were clothed in cloaks made from the hides of guanaco (an animal in the alpaca and llama family) and seals. They had dogs of a kind Banks perceived as being like an American breed that barked. The following day, while some of the men went hunting for seals, Banks and Solander set out in search of plants. Accompanying them were the ship's surgeon, William Monkhouse, astronomer Charles Green, several marines, two seamen and Banks's two African servants, Tom Richmond and George Dorlton. Banks's greyhound also went with them.

When they left on their expedition the weather was fine, but it soon turned to rain, wind and snow. As the snow became heavier, the party headed back towards the beach but the temperature continued to drop. Suffering from the cold and overcome with fatigue, Solander and Richmond both collapsed with exhaustion. It was getting dark, so Banks sent some men ahead to find a safe place where they could light a fire and settle for the night. Coaxed to their feet, Solander and Richmond only managed to go a little further before they again dropped into the snow. This time Richmond refused to get

Inhabitants of Tierra del Fuego, by Alexander Buchan. Wikimedia commons BL Add MS 23920

up, so Banks left him in the care of Dorlton and one of the seamen. Bonded to his master more than his owner, the greyhound refused to leave Richmond. Solander was assisted to his feet and sometimes dragged, sometimes carried, down the hill. Once Solander and the rest of the party reached the relative warmth and safety of a temporary camp, two men were sent back to help bring Richmond down. The men returned to the camp saying they could not find Banks's two servants, the seaman or the dog. For two hours it snowed incessantly, then around midnight, they heard someone shouting. It was the seaman. He reported Banks's two African servants were near death and led a party to where Richmond and Dorlton lay, the greyhound close to their frozen bodies. Distraught, they covered the bodies with branches and called the dog to follow them back to the camp. But again the loyal dog refused to leave Richmond. In despair the party trudged back to the warmth of the campfire. Shortly after, perhaps accepting that Richmond was no longer alive, the greyhound arrived and walked over to the fire.

When the snow stopped the distressed men and the dog returned to the ship. For several days Banks went off by himself to fish. Some interpreted Banks's behaviour as indifference to the death of his servant, but as Banks never caught any fish it is probable he went off to grieve in private. Banks never forgot the night that took the lives of his two servants. Once back in England he settled 'a pension upon a black woman, the wife of a faithful black servant who went with him, and perished by the cold of Terra del Fuego.'[12]

Keen to leave Tierra del Fuego behind and round Cape Horn, Cook ordered wood and water to be brought on board in readiness for recommencing their journey. It would be another four days before the winds changed in their favour.

Rounding Cape Horn

The conditions when sailing around Cape Horn were legendary. Cook was prepared for ferocious gales and turbulent seas. Instead they experienced long periods of calm. On 25 January 1769 *Endeavour* passed Cape Horn and entered the South Pacific Ocean. The voyage was relatively uneventful for the next two months. Until 26 March when private William Greenslade disappeared. Accused of theft by his peers, he was last seen running to the forecastle at the bow of the ship where he threw himself into the ocean. Cook was not informed for several hours. While it was too late to find and recover Greenslade's body, Cook was suspicious about the events that drove the quiet, industrious, twenty-one-year-old to commit suicide.

Questioning a number of people, Cook learnt that when Greenslade was on duty guarding the door of the Great Cabin (a precaution to prevent mutiny), one of Cook's servants left a piece of sealskin in his charge. Greenslade had wanted a sealskin tobacco pouch for a while, as they were a status symbol amongst the marines. He cut a piece off the sealskin. When the servant returned, he immediately saw what Greenslade had done. While he did not report the offence to Cook or to any of the other officers, the other marines soon came to know about it, and they accused him of dishonouring their corps. They exaggerated the theft as being an unforgiveable breach of trust. Sergeant Edgcumbe, a man highly respected by Cook,

threatened to report the theft to the captain. The marines taunted the sensitive young man with potential punishments that might be imposed on him. Later, when the sergeant told Greenslade to follow him to the upper deck, the terrified marine slipped past his superior and out of sight. Cook concluded William Greenslade committed suicide. His death was recorded, again without any evident emotion displayed by Cook.

Taking advantage of the moderate weather, the naturalists went out in one of the smaller boats to collect specimens of fish and seabirds. Banks took the greatest pleasure in shooting a light-mantled sooty albatross and a wandering albatross. Refusing to be intimidated by the mariners' superstitions around the killing of an albatross, Banks had his cook serve the wandering albatross for the gentlemen's dinner. Catching the albatrosses may not have endeared Banks to the sailors, but eating it must have fuelled their dislike of this wealthy, arrogant young man. In all probability the old mariners waited for some disaster to strike the ship. Instead, the southerly winds picked up and Cook was able to make a consistent north-westerly course.

They came to a small atoll to the east of Tahiti but were unable to find a safe anchorage there. Cook named it Lagoon Island (now called Vahitahi). If they had landed, they would not only have had access to a fortune in pearls, they would also have observed a unique species of dog that was covered in fine white hair.

Double canoes. Tipaerua. https://commons.wikimedia.org/wiki/File:Double_canoes._Tipaerua,_1769-71.jpg A. Buchan, S. Parkinson or J. F. Miller [Public domain]

Arriving at King George's Island (Otaheite)

On 13 April 1769 they sighted the stunningly beautiful island of Otaheite (Tahiti), named King George's Land by Samuel Wallis. Cook followed the course of *Dolphin*'s passage through the reef into Matavai Bay. The men who sailed on *Dolphin* less than two years earlier were keen to go on shore to renew old acquaintances. Perhaps recognising the area, the goat waited expectantly on the deck alongside the men. Seeing the goat was untied, an officer told Cook that one of the two nanny goats on *Dolphin* had caused a riot. When the Tahitian chief clambered over the rails, the goat had struck him on the buttocks. When the offended man spun around, the goat raised up onto her hind legs, ready to repeat the offence. The sight of the goat, a species he had never seen before, had struck the chief with such terror that he leapt overboard. His men, seeing their chief's fear, also jumped off the ship into the sea. Not wanting a repeat of Wallis's experience, Cook took the precautionary measure of ordering the goat tied up within sight of the Tahitians. Observing the old troublemaker secured to the railings, the chief, Owha'a, climbed up the side ladder as head of the welcoming committee, all smiles.

Cook was aware from Wallis's report that there were no goats, cattle or sheep in Tahiti. However, he expected to see an abundance of Polynesian pigs, dogs and junglefowl (chicken species that exist on many Pacific Islands from the Philippines to Easter Island). Cook was surprised to find only a few of these animals when they went on shore, and the few that were offered for trade were exorbitantly expensive. One old hog was offered in exchange for a hatchet, but Cook refused to trade, presenting one nail instead. The hog was taken away and days passed without any livestock being observed. Cook suspected the islanders had hidden them in the woods, but as it turned out, the French explorer Louis-Antoine de Bougainville had visited Tahiti a few months after Wallis. He acquired upwards of 800 fowls and 150 hogs.

The men were put to work setting up tents and building an observatory inside a protective fortification. On occasion the odd pig, dog or chicken would cross their path, but these were domesticated animals and not available for trade. Wandering around the island, the Englishmen came across animals and poultry housed on small estates, but again these were not for sale. With meat so scarce, Banks was delighted on one occasion to be served pork at a ceremonial feast, only to find the flesh of the introduced Chinese pig too fatty. The chicken Banks also found unpalatable, describing it as being very tough.[13] Another day, some of the gentlemen came across an immensely fat, tame English goose and an equally fat turkey cock, both having been left behind during *Dolphin*'s visit. This caused some excitement amongst the Europeans who anticipated a delicious feast, but both animals were kept close to their Tahitian owners, who were immensely fond of them.

On 16 April, Banks's artist Alexander Buchan suffered an epileptic seizure. It was so severe that a distraught Banks was told he would probably not survive and, sure enough, Buchan died the next day at 2 a.m. Buchan's death was a massive loss to Banks, not only because he was his landscape and portrait artist but also because Banks liked

Sketch by John Webber, from Anderson's A New, authentic, and complete collection of voyages round the world …, published for Alex. Hogg, London 1784.

and admired the young man. It was Buchan who had trekked in the snow at Tierra del Fuego on 16 January to find a suitable camp and light a fire for the frozen men. The loss of Buchan was not only a loss to Banks, his death was a blow to all the crew. The images created by Buchan and Parkinson are invaluable visual records of Cook's first exploration of the South Pacific.

It was decided to bury Buchan immediately, due to the heat and the persistent flies. At nine in the morning, fearing the islanders would be offended if they interred him on shore, the crew placed Buchan's body in the pinnace, where Cook conducted a brief service attended by Solander, Spöring, Parkinson and some of *Endeavour*'s officers. Buchan's corpse was then taken out to sea, weighted down and given a sailor's burial.[14]

Two chiefs, one they named Hercules on account of his size, came to commiserate with the English, bringing with them gifts of two hogs and two breadfruit. In return, they were each presented with a hatchet and a nail. A forge was set up to produce more of these highly desirable commodities and soon a brisk trade was under way. Coconuts and breadfruit were offered in abundance, but hogs continued to remain scarce. Desperate for fresh pork, the men travelled miles into the woods and along the beaches, but rarely did they see a wild pig. What had been an abundant resource only two years before the French reached Tahiti had almost vanished. Following Bougainville's insatiable desire for livestock, the only things in Tahiti that were plentiful when Cook first arrived there were the breadfruit, coconuts, ravenous flies and Polynesian rats.

A Feast of Tahitian Rats

(Rattus exulans) [en.wikipedia.org/wiki/Polynesian_rat]

While the Tahitians would eat the occasional poultry, domesticated pigs or dog, they would never eat the rats. Polynesian rats were prolific throughout Tahiti and became a source of entertainment for the seamen who would hunt them, easily killing a thousand a day. Robert Molyneux described lying in the woods with the rats playing about him 'as indifferent as about a Tree.' The seamen saw rats as dangerous pests and a potential food source on long voyages. They encouraged the Tahitians to add rat meat to their diet. When the islanders refused to eat the rodents, Cook decided to lead by example. He had his men hunt the rats; Cook ordered the meat to be fried or roasted and served to the Englishmen for their dinner. As they ate the so-called delicacies with exaggerated delight, portions were offered to the locals. But still the Tahitians would not eat the rats, and so once the officers had eaten their fill, the remainder was served to the lower officers for breakfast the next day.

Unable to figure out why the Tahitians would not eat the rats, the seamen decided it must be for religious reasons. The reality was the Tahitian people would not eat them because the rodents were the island's sewerage system.[15] There were no outhouses or long drops in Tahiti until the Europeans settled there, and the people would defecate at will in the knowledge the rats would clean up after them. Not only were the rats contaminated from eating human excrement, and therefore a health hazard, but if they had been eradicated there would have been a dangerous and detrimental effect on the island's established ecosystem. It was not religion but health underpinning the Tahitians' aversion to eating the rats. It can only be imagined what they thought of their visitors eating the filthy rodents with such enthusiasm. As there is no record of any of the seamen suffering from eating the rodents, it is possible Cook's example planted the seed of an idea that the vermin were edible.

TAHITIAN DOGS

While not as prolific as the rats, the Tahitian dogs were relatively plentiful. The Tahitian or 'Poe' dog first sighted by the European explorers (now extinct due to inbreeding with European dogs) was a small breed equal in size to a terrier. They were close relatives of other Polynesian dogs (including the kurī in New Zealand). The head was sharpened at the muzzle, the ears erect, the back long and the limbs crooked. Its tail was straight or slightly curved; the coat was smooth and a tan or rusty ochre colour. It was considered to be a lazy, silent animal that fed on a vegetable diet consisting predominantly of taro and breadfruit. The first known European to sketch the Poe dog, Parkinson, depicted the Tahitian dog in his sketch 'Double Canoes'.

While the Tahitian breed quickly became mongrelised, the Poe dog continued to

exist in the South Sandwich Islands in the South Atlantic until the mid-1800s. It was described by one explorer as being 'equal in size to a terrier, with a dull expression of countenance; tail straight or tightly curled, a brown livery and having a feeble but shrill bark; it is gentle, indolent, and in aspect presents the mixed forms of a fox-dog, turnspit and terrier'.[16]

In 1788, twenty years after Parkinson painted his image containing the Tahitian Poe dog, artist Charles Catton (the younger) created and published an etching of the Tahitian dog that he claimed was drawn from life (although he used a deceased animal as the model).

Rather than being as small as a terrier, Catton described the Poe dog as being about the size of a large spaniel and resembling them in appearance. In contrast to the spaniel, though, 'the head is rather longer and deeper, or flatter perpendicularly; the ears are erect like the wolf's; the limbs appear rather larger; the colour, for the most part, white, with lively brown spots or blotches'.[17] Given Catton's description, it is probable that the small terrier-like Tahitian Poe dog had been compromised by the introduction of European dogs within a period of two decades. Tahitian dogs were usually kept as pets rather than as a source of food, although on occasion were served during a ceremony involving someone in a prestigious position.

THE TRANSIT OF VENUS

As the date for the transit of Venus approached, clouds began to form. Cook took the precautionary measure of sending a small group of observers to the east and another party to the nearby Island of Imao

The Tahitian or Poe dog, sketched by Charles Catton, 1788

(or Eimeo, Duke of York's Island and now Mo'orea). Banks, Gore, William Monkhouse and a Tahitian priest by the name of Tupaia elected to go with the Imao expedition, crossing to the island a day before the expected occurrence. As they set up the observatory, the king of the island brought Banks a present of a hog, a dog and some breadfruit. In return, Banks presented the king with a shirt and some beads.

On 3 June 1769 each of the observation parties was able to see and record the transit of Venus crossing the face of the sun. The primary objective of the voyage now met, Cook opened sealed orders he had been given by the Admiralty when they left England. Rather than returning home, they were to continue southward in search of the undiscovered 'Great Southern Continent'.

In Search of New Lands

Perhaps because it was the middle of winter, six weeks would pass before Cook made his move. During this time he travelled around Tahiti with Banks and some of the other gentlemen, charting the coastline in detail and taking excursions inland. During one such excursion, Parkinson sketched a marae (a religious site) with a large hog being offered to the dead.

When they returned, the carpenters were ordered to take down the gates and posts of the fortification. *Endeavour* was loaded with casks of fresh water, yams, coconuts, small green bananas (plantains) and breadfruit. The animals that had been penned at the fort for three months were mustered on board, and a few pigs and poultry were added to sustain the men on the next part of the voyage. At his request, Tupaia, the Tahitian

priest, along with his young attendant, Tayeto, joined the expedition.

A heavily laden *Endeavour* sailed out of Tahiti on 13 July 1769, but within days, the pigs and poultry purchased at Tahiti began to die. Having only ever been fed fresh greens, they refused to eat the dried food that kept the English-bred animals alive. The planned exploration of the uncharted southern waters had little chance of success if there was insufficient food on board to maintain the men's health for a longer period. Therefore, Cook went in search of more provisions. Guided by Tupaia, *Endeavour* called into several neighbouring islands. First was Huahine, where they purchased twenty-four hogs and some smaller pigs. More were purchased at nearby islands, but it was not until they anchored at Ulietea (Ra'iātea), the last of what Cook would refer to as the Society Islands, that they were able to purchase as many hogs and bananas as they could stow.

On 9 August 1769, *Endeavour* left Ra'iātea and sailed southwards. The last of the poultry began to show symptoms of disease and were quickly slaughtered and eaten before it spread. The newly acquired island hogs survived well on the bananas, but by 21 August the bananas were gone and the pigs, refusing to eat the English grain, began to starve. Cook gave orders to slaughter and salt them. The men on *Endeavour* feasted on pork for a few weeks, then it was back to a seafarer's diet of biscuits, pease and sauerkraut.

Tupaia, who over the years had created his own map of the South Pacific islands, advised Cook that there was no Great Southern Continent to be found. Still, Cook followed his orders that directed him to sail as far south as latitude 40 degrees in search

A Marae with an offering to the Dead; Sydney Parkinson, July 1769. In Parkinson & Kenrick 1773.

of this mythical land. The further south they sailed, the worse the weather became. Gales ripped their sails and monstrous waves crashed and tore at *Endeavour*. Old repairs opened as the tired ship struggled to keep afloat. Reaching the desired latitude without sight of land and convinced there was no Great Southern Continent to be found in this part of the ocean, Cook turned his ship around. He decided to search for the land Abel Tasman had mapped and named over 120 years previously: Staten Land, later renamed Nova Zeelandia after the Dutch province of Zeeland. (James Cook would anglicise the name to New Zealand.)

Two weeks before they came in sight of land, a concerned Banks itemised the livestock they had left on board: seventeen sheep, four or five fowl, the same number of Tahitian pigs, four or five Muscovy ducks, one English boar and an English sow with a litter of piglets.[18] Not knowing when they might sight land and be able to obtain fresh supplies, Cook ordered the remaining animals to be used only in an emergency. The men's diet would now consist of sauerkraut, portable soup (similar to today's stock cubes) and their seemingly endless supply of essence of wort (a yeast-based product similar to Marmite).

Towards the end of September, they observed floating debris and land birds, both signs of land being nearby. In celebration, they slaughtered and roasted a sheep. At the feast, Cook promised one gallon of rum to the man who first spotted land, and two gallons if the man discovered it during the night. As an extra incentive, Cook announced the part of the coast first observed would be named after the man who spotted it. For

days, all eyes became fixed on the horizon, but it was not until 5 October, at about two o'clock in the afternoon, that the surgeon's boy on *Endeavour*, eleven-year-old Nicholas Young, made his claim. Swinging from the masthead, he screamed out 'Land!' By the time the sun began to set, everyone on board had glimpsed it. They celebrated that evening, the land (Te Ūpoko-o-te-kurī-a-Paoa) was called Young Nick's Head and the boy received his reward of rum. He would have been popular amongst the sailors that night.

First Arrival in New Zealand

Searching for a safe harbour, they sailed along the east coast, keeping close to the shore.

Desperate for fresh water and food, on the afternoon of Sunday, 8 October 1769, *Endeavour* entered a large bay, where they observed several canoes with people in them. At the head of the bay was a river. On a hill above the river were a cluster of huts, and next to the huts was an enclosure surrounded by a fence. Banks speculated the fence surrounded either a deer park or a paddock of oxen and sheep. Excited with anticipation, Cook, Banks, Solander, Tupaia and some of the crew, escorted by several marines, went out in the yawl and pinnace. They landed on the shore below the hill, next to the mouth of the river (Gisborne's Tūranganui River). On the opposite bank stood a group of Māori, who made it clear they did not welcome the intruders. Keeping a safe distance from the group, Cook and his party went on shore, leaving four young sailors to guard the boats. While they were gone, four Māori rushed

First sighting of New Zealand, Saturday, 7th October 1769. Artist: Alan Sanders ©2017

to the beach to seize the yawl. Cook's boys panicked. Sailors in the pinnace rushed to the boys' assistance. They fired at the Māori and shot the leader through the heart. Cook's party heard the rifle shot and rushed back to the beach.

The men returned to the shore the next day, to face a group of over fifty hostile Māori. Baffled by the reception, so unlike the welcome they received on the Pacific islands, Cook decided to capture some Māori and convince them they were friendly. Seeing two canoes returning from fishing, Cook tried enticing them to *Endeavour*. When the fishermen ignored the invitation, Cook had a shot fired over their heads. The Māori responded by attacking the ship with their own weapons. Cook ordered his men to fire again and some of the Māori were killed. Three others, young men who were merely boys, the youngest about ten, jumped into the sea and were taken on board *Endeavour* as prisoners. Noting their distress and seeking to console the boys, Tupaia spoke to them softly in his own language. To everyone's amazement, the boys understood him, and Tupaia was able to translate what they said. When questioned about what food was available, they told them 'there was Taro, Eape (Rapeseed plant), Oomara (Kumara), Yams, and also a peculiar kind of Deer, to be found upon the island.'[19] However, there were no deer, oxen, sheep, or any other species of domestic livestock in New Zealand. That Parkinson thought the boys

New Zealand war canoe bidding defiance to the ship.' From the British Museum's collection of drawings by A. Buchan, S. Parkinson and J. F. Miller, 1768-71). Ref. No: Add. Ms. 23920f.50. Record No.: 20260

said there were deer was probably a result of confusion in the translation.

The three boys were fed mutton, which they recoiled from, thinking it was human flesh. To reassure them, they were shown the sheep penned on the upper deck. The sight of the sheep alarmed them, and they indicated they had never seen animals that large before. Cook returned the boys to the shore. Disappointed at the unfriendly welcome and having found no fresh provisions, Cook named the bay Poverty Bay (called Tūranganui-a-Kiwa by Māori).

Exiting the bay, they continued on a southerly course in search of what they hoped would be a more bountiful anchorage. Keeping close to the coastline, they observed areas of cultivated land and vast numbers of people watching them from the high cliffs. Without warning, the bottom of *Endeavour* scraped against some rocks. Cook ordered a small boat lowered to check the depth of

water. While the sailors were away from their ship, some canoes pushed off from the beach and advanced towards them. Seeing warriors shouting and making threatening gestures, Cook ordered an officer to fire a musket. The sailors quickly clambered back on board and all but one very large canoe, carrying about twenty armed, hostile men, withdrew. Parkinson immortalised the war party in a drawing.

Clearly shown in the centre of the canoe is a white or light-coloured dog. It is a small

Māori Dogs (Kurī)

While Parkinson described the Māori dogs as 'being like those on the island of Otaheite',[20] there were some differences between those they observed on Tahiti and the New Zealand breed. Both had a relatively large head in comparison to the body, remarkably little eyes, prick-ears, long hair and a short bushy tail. But the New Zealand dog appeared more like a fox, and some were spotted, some were black and some were white.[21] They were considered by the seamen to be stupid and lazy animals that cried rather than barked and were only suited as food or their pelt as a resource to decorate clothing worn by Māori. Banks simply described the New Zealand dog as being 'very small and ugly.'[22]

Dogs played a key role in the pre-European Māori economy. It was food, predominantly a 'luxury reserved for important personages'[23] and provided skin and tufts of fur for the Māori cloak. Never prolific in numbers, today the kurī is extinct, primarily because of interbreeding with introduced breeds of dogs. There is a bitch mounted at New Zealand's national museum,

Collected 1876, between "Waikawa" & Mataura plains, Catlins, New Zealand. Gift of Mr Anderson, 1876. CC BY-NC-ND 4.0. Te Papa (LM000828). Permission granted by National Museum of New Zealand Te Papa Tongarewa

Te Papa Tongarewa, that in the 1880s was acknowledged by several elderly Māori as a genuine kurī or ancient Māori dog. Having been observed chasing sheep, the bitch and her full-grown pup were shot in the densely wooded country between Waikawa and the Mataura plains in the lower South Island. Their bodies were presented to the Colonial Museum and later the younger dog's skin and skeleton were given to the British Museum by Sir George Grey.

However, their authenticity as purebred kurī has since been disputed.

William Colenso, a printer, missionary, naturalist and explorer,[24] arrived at the Bay of Islands in December 1834. Intrigued by the stories from Māori elders of a small, highly prized, indigenous white dog that did not bark, or bite men, and which was trained to hunt ground birds for their masters, he resolved to find one. Despite trekking across the North Island in search of the Māori dog, 'from Cook Strait to Cape Maria Van Diemen' from 1834 to 1854, visiting Māori pā (forts) and villages, he never came across one. He did, however, obtain in 1835 physical evidence of their existence: 'An ancient, large, and handsome chief's staff and weapon of defence (a taiha), which was richly ornamented with carving, red feathers from under the wings of the parrot (*Nestor meridionalis*), and the flowing hair of the old Maori dog.' This hair, apparently, was 'long, fine, and white, beautifully and securely done up in little queues having their ends firmly bound round with the finest spun flax.'[25]

Colenso came across a large number of dogs in his early travels that he thought were either a crossbred kurī or a breed from the South Pacific islands, but none fully matched the description he knew to be characteristic of the ancient Māori dog. It was Colenso's conclusion that the kurī had died out through crossbreeding in the late eighteenth century. His findings also led him to declare the two dogs caught in the lower South Island to be hybrids: a cross between the kurī and European dogs.

animal with pointed ears, long pointed face, black nose, a rat-like tail and short spindly legs that support a plump body. Parkinson's image is the first drawing of a Māori dog (kurī) by a European. In the sketch the animal appears to be unconstrained, suggesting the dog was more than just a source of food and clothing to Māori.

Ngai Tuhoe elder wearing a Huia and Kiwi feather cloak. Pastel by Phillip Waddington (Author's collection).

A Kidnapping

Towing the small boat behind *Endeavour*, they circled Māhia Peninsula, entered Hawke's Bay and continued a slow exploration down the east coast of the North Island (Te Ika-a-Māui). Māori would often approach them, either warning them threateningly to move on or offering fish for trade. One large canoe, holding about twenty-two armed men, approached *Endeavour*. While they had nothing to trade, Cook thought it prudent to give them some pieces of cloth. Accepting the gift, the Māori immediately demanded more. Reluctant to hand additional items to the warriors without receiving something in return, Cook offered some red cloth for a black skin cloak one of the men was wearing. The man removed his cloak and offered it to Cook, holding out his other hand for the red cloth. When Cook released the red cloth, the Māori thrust the cloth and the cloak into a basket at his feet, and the canoe speedily departed the ship. Cook chose to ignore this incident.

A short time later, while they were trading with a small canoe offering fish, the offending canoe returned. Several men in the large canoe grabbed Tupaia's boy, Tayeto, who was over the side collecting fish. Two Māori held him down while others feverishly paddled for the shore, the accompanying canoes racing off after them. The marines, always on standby during these trading sessions, fired a shot into the canoe that held the terrified boy. The startled warriors released Tayeto, who leapt into the ocean and frantically swam towards the ship. The marines continued to fire their muskets, and Cook ordered one of the big guns to fire at the largest canoe. Some marines dragged Tayeto on board to safety. Cook named this place Cape Kidnappers (Te Kauae-o-Māui). While Cook referred to the cloak in this incident as being black and probably a bearskin, William Monkhouse described it as being a brown colour bordered in white. Banks later identified the cloak as being dog fur that had been cut into long strips and sewn onto dogskin.[26] Banks was partially correct. What the Europeans initially perceived as bearskin was in all probability dogskin decorated with the feathers of kiwi, pūkeko and kākāpo birds, edged by strips of dog fur.[27]

Friendly Welcome at Tolaga Bay

They continued their journey south as far as Cape Turnagain (Te Poroporo). Pounded by a southerly wind, Cook turned back towards the north. Now desperate for fresh water, they braved the surf at Anaura Bay, landing a boat by two shallow streams. While they were laboriously filling casks with water, a group of Māori, accompanied by a great many dogs with small pointed ears, cautiously approached them. The group said there was better access to fresh drinking water in a bay a little further back to the south. Heeding their advice, they sailed south to Tolaga Bay (Uawa). Cook, Banks, several gentlemen, some marines and Tupaia went ashore and approached a group of males who challenged them with a haka (ceremonial war dance). Tupaia called out to them in the Tahitian language, which they understood. The Māori stopped their haka and welcomed Cook's party. Tupaia's ability to translate, his charismatic presence alongside Cook, along with his calm demeanour, undoubtedly influenced the success of Cook's first exploration of New Zealand.

With easy access to fresh water and a brisk trade of fish, yams and sweet potatoes, Cook decided to stay in this friendly bay. For several days he was able to relax and familiarise himself with the country and its wildlife. On 29 October 1769, while moored at Tolaga Bay, Cook wrote, 'we saw no 4 footed Animals, either Tame or Wild, or signs of any, except Dogs and Rats.' He later commented that the rats were so scarce in New Zealand when they arrived that not only he, but also many others in the ship, never saw one.

Leaving Tolaga Bay

Before leaving Tolaga Bay, Cook gave to Māori two grey cats and two dogs. Te Apaapaoterangi, a Tāranganui chief, said 'the cat was a new animal which was brought by the Pakeha. … Puhi [pussy] was the female and Kati [cat] was the male.'[32] The cats soon ran off into the forest, but the dogs remained with the tribe. Te Apaapaoterangi described the dogs as black with projecting ears and white chests. It is likely they were dogs picked up in Tahiti, or were young dogs sired by Banks's greyhound and born on *Endeavour*.

Polynesian Rats/kiore

The New Zealand rat (*Rattus exulans*), now known as the kiore, Pacific or Polynesian rat, was introduced by migrating Polynesians. They contributed to the survival of early Māori, as prior to the introduction of pigs and other livestock, they were an important item in the Māori diet.[28] When first introduced, the kiore lived predominantly on fruit and made its home on the branches of the tawhai (silver beech, *Nothofagus menziesii*) tree.[29] However, as an omnivore it soon adapted to its new environment and became a menace to the eggs and chicks of indigenous birds, as well as to insects, lizards and other wildlife.

Mus Novae Zelandiae. Wikimedia Commons

Now relatively uncommon in New Zealand, the kiore can be distinguished from the two species introduced later by Europeans: the brown (or Norway) rat (*Rattus norvegicus*) and the black rat (*Rattus rattus*; also known as the English, roof, plague, house or ship rat), by its smaller size and thin, dark tail.[30] In marked contrast to the kiore, which has a tail similar in length to its head and tail, the black rat has a tail considerably longer than its body. While the brown rat has a tail similar in length to the kiore, it can be identified by its ears which, unlike the kiore, do not cover its eyes when pulled forward.[31]

As they continued up the east coast of New Zealand, into the Bay of Plenty, they were repeatedly approached by canoes, sometimes laden with items to trade, at other times carrying men waving pikes and lances at them or throwing stones.

Early in November, they settled in a large bay (Te Whanganui-a-Hei, named Mercury Bay by Cook) where they observed the transit of Mercury. Cook continued to explore various landing sites, including a river (Waihou) that he would name after the Thames in England.

Further north, at the Bay of Islands, four huge canoes approached *Endeavour* and the occupants threw freshly caught fish onto her deck. Each canoe was commanded by a chief. *Te Tumuaki*, the first canoe, was manned by eighty men under the command of Tapua. Cook invited the four chiefs on board and gave them gifts that included European garments and some of their last pork.[33] Tapua had a son, Patuone, who lived to be 108 years old. Patuone recalled watching *Endeavour* from the beach: 'I saw Cook's vessel … my father received presents of garments, and brought with him to the shore a cooked joint of pork, which was eaten by myself and sister Tari. This was the first time we Maoris had seen the flesh of a pig.'[34]

They continued their journey towards the north. On 9 December 1769, while *Endeavour* was stationary outside Doubtless Bay (Ōruru), a number of Māori approached them wanting to trade. Cook and Banks urged Tupaia to ask them if they had livestock. When Tupaia asked them if they had pigs they told him no, but that some of their people had sailed away in a very big canoe. They were gone for a long time. Some of them returned and reported that, after sailing for a month (they indicated

a direction towards the north-west), they came across a country where the inhabitants ate an animal, which they called 'booah'. Tupaia asked if they brought the boars back with them. When they said no, Tupaia accused them of lying. He said their ancestors would never have been such fools as to leave something as important as pigs behind. The group could not have been offended by Tupaia's allegation, as they returned that evening with more fish to trade. The Māori told them they were about three days rowing from 'Moorewhennua' (Muriwhenua), which Cook took to be Cape Maria van Diemen. Near North Cape (Ōtū), they sailed into a powerful storm. Facing gales of a force they had rarely experienced before, Cook sought the safety of the open sea.

THE FRENCH ARRIVE IN NEW ZEALAND

Unbeknown to Cook, this same violent storm blew a Frenchman, Jean-François-Marie de Surville, towards New Zealand. A week after Cook departed New Zealand, de Surville's ship, *St Jean Baptiste*, rounded North Cape and sailed into Doubtless Bay. Māori cautiously approached the badly damaged ship to find most of the Frenchmen in a pitiful state. Sixty of de Surville's men had died of scurvy and the rest were emaciated and in various stages of dying. As a sympathetic chief wrapped the ailing commander in a dogskin coat, de Surville turned to Guillaume Labé, his first officer, and said, 'I think we are saved.'[35]

When their health was restored, a grateful de Surville invited their rescuers to join them for a meal of roast pork. Delighted with the meat, the chief asked for some live pigs, but rather than give up the pigs, de Surville gave the chief their last cock and a hen. These were small white Siamese bantams with feathery legs.

The Frenchmen showed no signs of preparing to return to sea. Apprehensive the seamen might be contemplating settling on their land, the Māori chief began to question how long his visitors planned to stay. Aware the mood of their host was changing towards them, de Surville offered the chief a breeding pair of small pigs. A few days later, on 26 December, Labé gave a second breeding pair of small pigs to a chief residing in a cul-de-sac they named Refuge Cove (Patia-Matariki Beach). Having outstayed their welcome, the Frenchmen kidnapped a Ngāti Kahu chief, Ranginui, and sailed for Peru. Ranginui died of scurvy on 24 March, and de Surville met his death two weeks later, drowning in the surf on 8 April 1770. While Cook may have been the first European to step onto New Zealand's shores, with the introduction of the pigs and bantams, de Surville was the first European to introduce livestock into New Zealand.

DE SURVILLE'S SECRET VOYAGE

On 3 March 1769, with a crew of 172 men and on the pretence of heading for China's Canton (Guangzhou), the French ship *St Jean Baptiste* sailed down the Hooghly River and into the Bay of Bengal. Her commander, Jean-Francois-Marie de Surville, was sailing under secret orders to find and claim for the French a South Pacific island rumoured to be rich in resources. The rumour had evidently been generated at the Cape of Good Hope. After his expedition to Tahiti on *Dolphin* in 1767, Wallis anchored in Table Bay at the Cape of Good Hope to refresh his men and repair his ship before returning home to England. While *Dolphin*'s officers had been instructed to hand in their diaries and journals to their captain, the ordinary sailors, most of whom were in their teens and twenties, spilled their stories of their adventures, with some embellishment, in the local grog shops.

Arriving at Yanaon, de Surville purchased livestock to sustain the men for the next part of their journey: fourteen bullocks, fifty-four kids and 750 heads of poultry. A week later they anchored in Masulipatnam where they bought a few more bullocks, hens and sheep. Their next stop was Pondicherry; this would be their last port of call in India. On 29 June they arrived at Malacca, a town populated by the Dutch, Malays and Chinese. Livestock purchased here were buffalo and poultry. Their next ports of call included Pulo (Palau) Tioman, where they were only able to refresh their water, followed by Trengannu (Terengganu, in the Gulf of Thailand), where they bought all manner of goods, including hens, large and small bullocks and some buffalo. They continued on a normal course for a ship bound for Canton, but to the surprise of his officers, de Surville ordered a change of direction to the east.

As they traversed the South China Sea, their provisions ran out and the last buffalo died. Still de Surville kept on an east by north-east course. At last, in the middle of

August, he steered them towards the isolated Bashi Islands that lie between Taiwan and the Philippines. There they anchored and filled their water casks. They also purchased pigs, goats and fresh vegetables, which were plentiful and cheap. With his ship now laden with provisions, de Surville steered on a south-easterly course. For weeks they sailed, their dwindling water supply being refreshed by the occasional squall.

The men began to complain of stomach pains and swollen gums: clear symptoms of scurvy. De Surville stopped chicken being served at the officers' table and the poultry were used in a broth brewed for the sick. Men were put on watch in the hope they would glimpse the shape of an island on the horizon, but for weeks the sea continued to be empty. As they crossed the tropics, food and water became even more tightly rationed. The heat became unbearable, the number of sick increased and the ailing men were left to lie in their own vomit as there was no one strong enough to care for them. Only the vermin thrived. 'Cockroaches bred in the damp penumbra and crept over clothes and food, while down in the hold rats gnawed at the cargo.'

After crossing the equator without the usual fanfare, land was sighted. They had stumbled upon the Solomon Islands, green and inviting, situated to the east of the Molucca Islands. But rather than finding rescue, they were attacked by hundreds of terrified islanders. Desperate for fresh water, de Surville ordered the capture of a young boy and, under threat of death, the lad led them to a freshwater stream. Armed with guns, they quickly filled their barrels with water, all the while keeping a wary eye on the islanders watching them from the forest. Struggling with the water barrels, some hastily scavenged firewood and palm cabbages, they returned to their ship. These meagre supplies were not enough to counteract the effects of scurvy and the weakest men died.

Despite the horrific state of those on board, de Surville refused to stop at any of the islands they passed in fear of further attacks or being wrecked on the reefs. Twenty-nine of de Surville's men had now died and many more were seriously ill. With such a high mortality rate, there would soon be insufficient crew to operate the ship. De Surville referred to his charts and Abel Tasman's account of his voyage in 1642. He called the officers together and said they would make for Tasman's 'Nova Zeelandia'. Each day more men died, until, on 12 December 1769, a man sitting in the crow's nest struggled to his feet and cried 'Land!' But the terrain they approached was just a long line of sand dunes. 'It was, though they knew it not, Hokianga Harbour and the sandy hills of western Northland.' De Surville gave the order to sail north in search of a more agreeable harbour, but instead of a safe haven, they sailed into a storm. This was the same storm that was blowing *Endeavour* out to sea.

Endeavour in Queen Charlotte Sound. Sherrin & Wallace 1890: 32

ENDEAVOUR RETURNS TO NEW ZEALAND

For three weeks *Endeavour* was at the mercy of the prevailing winds and tides. On 24 December they spotted what they thought were the Three Kings Islands off the northern tip of New Zealand. The sea was calm, so Banks went out in a small boat and shot some large white gannets, which Banks called solan Geese. On Christmas day the men were served with goose pie and, following the tradition of mariners before them, got horribly drunk.

Two more weeks passed as they slowly made their way down the west coast of New Zealand's North Island. The only event to excite the men was an experiment trialled by Banks. On 6 January 1770 the weather was calm and the sea flat, so a couple of the men, including Banks, were out in the small boat. Two albatrosses were seen sitting quietly on the water. Banks had been told that an albatross was unable to take flight on a calm sea, and decided to test the theory. Says Banks, 'one I shot dead, the other who was near him swam off near as fast as my small boat could row; we gave chase and came up a little.' The albatross attempted to fly 'by taking the moment of a waves falling but did not succeed. I who was so far off that I knew I could not hurt him fired at him to make his attempts more vigorous, which had the effect for the third effort he got upon the wing, tho I believe had it not been for a little swell upon the water he could not have done it.'

More excitement swept around the ship on 12 January. A high peak, covered in snow, was sighted. Cook named it Mount Egmont (Taranaki). Around the base of the mountain were what appeared to be flocks of sheep, although on closer inspection they saw the white shapes were just large stones. On the evening of 14 January, they stood outside the bay named Murderers Bay (Golden Bay/Mohua) by Abel Tasman. While they intended to go into the bay the next morning, the wind blew them towards the east.

Their fresh meat almost exhausted, *Endeavour* entered Cook Strait (Raukawa Moana) on 15 January 1770, and sailed into the sheltered harbour of Queen Charlotte Sound (Tōtaranui). Despite the winds being mild and variable, the currents carried the ship too close to the shore. The small boats towed her off and Cook had *Endeavour* securely anchored in a small cove (Meretoto) that he named Ship Cove.

They were soon surrounded by Māori who paddled around the ship 'defying and threatening us as usual and at last hove some stones aboard which we all expected to be a prelude of some behaviour which would oblige us to fire upon them.'[36] One old man tried to climb on board *Endeavour*, so they hauled him up and gave him some presents. The watching Māori broke into a haka then departed when the elderly man returned to them.

On Cook's orders the men disembarked, unloaded supplies and established a camp near a small stream. Concerned for the remaining animals on *Endeavour*, Banks reminded Cook that the livestock had not received fresh fodder since leaving the Society Islands five months earlier. Finding little grass in the cove, Cook sent men out in the longboat in search of fresh greens for the starving animals.

The following afternoon, while most of the crew were engaged in either repairing

QUEEN CHARLOTTE SOUND
Arapawa Island

Okoha Saddle
Endeavour Inlet
Mt Furneaux 823
Cannibal Cove
Te Ahitaore
Motuara Island
Ship Cove
Cape Koamaru
Ngatunutoru
Te Huainua Bay
Opou Pt
Oamaru Bay
Te Ariori Pt
The Brothers
Kokomohua Islands
Ekiera
Te Ruatanore
The Twins
Motungarara Is.
Umukorota Bay
Tewhaimoa
Big Bay
Long Island
Cooper Pt
Paparoa Pt
Tungougo
Kipirita
Camp Bay
Resolution Bay
Battle Rock
Kotukutuku
Papatoia
Onehunga Bay
Ruapawa Bay
Endeavour Inlet
Tawa Bay
Whatapu
Anatohia Bay
Onario Pt
Papakura Pt
Nukuna Bay
Pinottoi Pt
Onanhu Bay
Manne Head
Scott Pt
Clark Pt
Wharekupengas Bay
Papakura Bay
Deep Bay
Bakers Bay
Edgecombe Pt
Blumine Island (Oruawairua)
East Bay
Otonga Pt
Bald Hill 258
Awash Rock
uru Head
Toenga 467
Mint Bay
Dryden Bay
Pickersgill Island
Parea Pt
Fitzgerald Bay
Otaneran Bay
Lip Valley
510
Huru
Longfellow Bay
Kunakuna Pt
Wharehunga Bay (Grass Cove)
Burneys Beach
Puru Bay
Te Aroha Bay
Arapawa Island
Spenser Bay
Bay of Many Coves (Miritu Bay)
Amerikiwhati Is.
Te Ipapakereru Bay
Waikakenamua Bay
Arapawa 485
Narawha 559
Snake Pt
Queen Charlotte Sound (Totaranui)
Ahurmakiti Bay
Perano Head
Raukawa Rock
Bull Head
West Head
Dombie Bay
Umurukeke Bay
Cook's Lookout
Wairere 435
Okukari Bay
Te Awaiti Bay
East Head
West Head
Kaituhat Bay
Kaitapeha 387
Ahuroru Bay
Deep Bay
Tipi Bay
ffenbach Pt
Te Iro Bay
Winnuaka Pt
Tory Channel
Te Rua Bay
Maraetai Bay
Hitaua Bay
Onapua Bay
Erie Bay
Maoro Is.
Te Weuweu Bay
Te Pangu Bay
Tio Pt
Oyster Bay
Jordy Rocks

Captain Cook narrowly averted disaster on February 6th 1770 when the wind dropped and the Endeavour was nearly carried onto The Brothers by a rip tide.

Captain James Cook entered Queen Charlotte Sound and landed at Ship Cove on the 16th January 1770. The Endeavour was careened, and on Motuara Island Cook claimed the Sound together with adjacent territories in the name of King George III.

Cook spent a total of 100 days at Ship Cove visiting on five separate occasions over the course of his three voyages.

On his second voyage (1773/74) Cook commanded the Resolution, accompanied by the Adventure under Captain Furneaux. During this voyage a party of 10 sailors from the Adventure was attacked, killed and eaten by Maori in Wharehunga Bay, Arapawa Island.

On Cook's final voyage (1777), the Resolution was accompanied by the Discovery under Captain Clerke.

On 7 February 1838, Ngati Toa (under Te Rauparaha) clashed with their former allies Te Atiawa in Te Awaiti Bay. The fight was inconclusive despite considerable loss of life.

0 1 2 3 4 5 km

Endeavour or fishing, Cook, Banks, Solander and Tupaia, accompanied by some marines, took the pinnace to explore along the coast. They rowed about a mile to the north of their landing place when they came across what they thought was a dead seal floating on the water. As they got closer, they saw it was the decomposing body of a woman. The men left the corpse and continued to a cove where they found a family of Māori. Most of the people ran away, except an old man and a child. The old man said the dead woman was a relative and it was their custom to tie a stone to the dead and throw them into the sea. The men looked at the oven where they were told a dog was being cooked. Near the oven were some baskets. Inside one of the baskets were two bones that were undoubtedly human. While they suspected Māori were cannibals, this was the first time any of them were confronted with evidence of cannibalism. Horrified, the men clambered into their boat and quickly joined the others at Ship Cove. The bay they left behind them was Anaho; Cook named it Cannibal Cove. With the marines fully armed and alert, the Europeans settled into a routine of trading with Māori, repairing *Endeavour*, gathering provisions and exploring the northern end of Queen Charlotte Sound.

On 22 January, Cook, Banks and Solander, accompanied by some seamen and armed marines, landed on the western side of Arapawa Island (Arapaoa Island). Leaving the two scientists collecting plants near the shore, Cook and a sailor climbed the nearby hill (probably Kaitapeha) to view their surroundings. From this vantage point Cook incorrectly assumed Arapawa Island was part of the mainland. On Wednesday 31 January 1770, Cook set up a post in Ship Cove and hoisted the Union flag. Inscribed on the post was the name of his ship, the month and the year. He, Tupaia and William Monkhouse took a similar post across to Motuara Island. There they met the old man who had climbed on *Endeavour*. Cook explained the purpose of the post was to show any future ship that called into the sound that they had been here before. The old man, who they would later refer to as Goubiah (also Ko Paea or Kupia),[37] gave his consent to set up the post, and promised to never pull it down.

They stayed in Queen Charlotte Sound for three weeks. With the men and remaining livestock restored to health, and *Endeavour* repaired and loaded with dried fish, fresh water and greens, Cook decided it was time to continue their search for the Great Southern Land.

Endeavour sailed out of the Sound towards the east on 6 February. They turned to the north until they recognised Cape Turnagain in the distance. Satisfied that the North Island was indeed an island, they turned back and commenced the circumnavigation of New Zealand's South Island, Te Waipounamu. Sailing down the east coast, they passed what appeared to be an island but was actually a peninsula on the mainland (Horomaka or Te Pātaka o Rākaihautū). Cook named it Banks Peninsula after his shipmate, an action that reflected friendship between the two men.

As they approached the Otago Peninsula, a gale forced them out to sea. On their return to land, *Endeavour* narrowly avoided being dashed on a reef at the south end of Stewart Island/Rakiura. Cook aptly named the reef

'The Traps'. Mistaking Foveaux Strait for a bay, they rounded the southern cape of New Zealand on 10 March 1770. With no new large mass of land in sight, it was time to return home to England. In celebration of a junior officer's birthday, they resorted to eating a young dog that had been bred on *Endeavour*: 'the hindquarters roasted, a pie made of the forequarters, and the entrails turned into a haggis.'[38]

As they sailed up the South Island's west coast, Cook hovered outside the opening to a dusky, hazy bay, and mapped what he perceived would make a good harbour. Because of the high winds, he decided it would be unwise to enter the fiord and so they continued northward. They sailed past cliffs that rose up from the sea, mountains rising up behind them covered with snow. This was a reminder that winter was approaching in the southern hemisphere.

In six months of circumnavigating New Zealand, the only four-legged animals they saw were Māori dogs and the occasional rat.

Bustard, Rees 1820: Fig 28

When they left New Zealand on Saturday, 31 March 1770, the remaining animals on board, apart from unwelcome vermin, were Banks's dogs, the ship's cats, some pigs that were probably of Polynesian origin, a few English sheep and the little English milking goat.

EXPLORING THE EAST COAST OF AUSTRALIA

With southerlies pushing *Endeavour* to the north, on 29 April 1770 Cook took shelter in an inlet on the east coast of New Holland (Australia). Impressed by the large quantity of plants that Banks and Solander gathered, as well as the exquisite beauty of the birds, Cook named the inlet Botany Bay.

Exploring inland, they came across a four-legged animal that was about the size of a rabbit. Banks's greyhound, chasing after it, hurt his leg when he ran into a stump concealed in the long grass. While they observed no other quadruped in this area, they did come across evidence that some were around: 'we found the dung of an animal that must feed upon grass and which we judged could not be less than a deer, we also saw the track of a dog or some such Animal.'[39] While the dung could have come from a kangaroo or some other marsupial they were yet to discover, a dingo may have left the track or it could have been the now-extinct thylacine (commonly referred to as the Tasmanian tiger or wolf).

Finding the few Aboriginals they met had no interest either in *Endeavour* or their trinkets, Cook ordered fresh water and hay be loaded on board, raised the English flag and had an inscription carved into a tree.

On 23 May they anchored in a bay close to the mouth of a large lagoon. In search of fresh produce, they took small boats up the inlet, running into swamps and bogs of salt water. On the banks of the lagoon were mangrove trees, and on the branches of the trees were numerous nests of ants. When the men disturbed the branches, bright-green ants dropped down and attacked them (probably the green tree/weaver ant). Ridding themselves of the biting ants, they continued inland, coming across some small, equally green, caterpillars. A fascinated Banks said there would be twenty or thirty of these hairy little creatures sitting on one leaf, lined up side by side like soldiers. As the men reached out to touch the caterpillars, they found the little hairs on the insects to be like stinging nettles. (These caterpillars are the larvae of the Australian cup moth). They left them alone and continued looking for food and fresh water.

During this excursion, they came across some large birds that they perceived to be like a pelican, and some others, less shy, that they were able to get close enough to shoot. A large bustard (a terrestrial bird that lives in the grasslands) was shot and later eaten. Cook was so delighted with the meat he named the place Bustard Bay. While they were trawling for fish amongst the mangrove trees, their net became damaged and so they returned to *Endeavour*. Back on board they discovered a group of about twenty Aboriginals had been standing on the beach studying the ship. Concerned the men might be planning to attack them, Cook gave the order to raise the anchor and they returned to sea. Less than a week later, they entered another bay. Cook named this place Thirsty Sound, as there was no fresh water to be found. Here there were gum trees with branches that had large nests made of rough clay. Rather than birds, the nests contained swarms of small ants with white abdomens.

Endeavour on the reef — 11th June 1770. In King 1891: facing page 13. Accessed Dec. 2018, Alexander Turnbull Library, P910.4, Cook, KIN, 1892 (1812)

After several more excursions around the nearby coastline, they continued northwards. At one point they became trapped between the land and the ocean by the Great Barrier Reef. On 11 June, *Endeavour* impaled on some coral and part of her keel ripped off. Attempting to float their ship off the reef, they threw overboard all heavy items considered expendable. Cannons, casks, ballast and decayed stores were thrown into the sea. Despite their efforts, *Endeavour* began to sink. Every man on board knew there were not enough boats to ensure the survival of everyone. In fear for their lives, it was all hands to the pump, including the captain and the gentlemen.

To everyone's relief, *Endeavour* dislodged from the coral and the changing tide floated her off the reef. However, they were still in danger. Lodged in the hull was a huge piece of coral. The ship was badly torn and water poured in faster than they could bail it out. In desperation Cook, on the advice of experienced Midshipman Jonathan Monkhouse, agreed to try the old mariners' method of 'fothering the ship'. Monkhouse ordered the men to mix together untwisted fibre from old ropes with hair and sheep's wool. They chopped it up small, then stuck handfuls of it loosely onto a sail laid out on the deck. Thrown over top of the chopped fibre was animal manure and all the other gluey filth they could gather. Men trampled over the mess to compress it, then following Monkhouse's instruction attached ropes so they could haul the prepared sail under *Endeavour*'s keel. Incoming water sucked the treated sail up into the hole. This temporarily blocked the leak. Men went into the boats and tried to tug *Endeavour* towards the beach. But as the ship moved, she turned onto her side.

They were in danger of losing the tiller, the platform that had been built over it, and the sheep pens connected to the platform. They stopped towing; their survival was now in the hands of the gods. When the tide turned, the platform broke and the empty sheep pens fell into the sea, but the tiller was saved. The sea quietened, allowing them enough time to get *Endeavour* safely ashore. When they hauled her onto the beach and saw the magnitude of the damage, the men attributed their deliverance to the sheep's fibre: 'in the midst of all their joy for their unexpected deliverance, they had not forgotten that there was nothing but a lock of wool between them and destruction.'[40]

Kangaroo Pennant No. 229 (Alexander Turnbull Library, Wellington)

It would take days for the carpenters to put temporary patches on *Endeavour*, so several gentlemen used the time to explore the countryside in search of fresh water and food. On 23 June they came across a mouse-coloured, slender animal that had a long tail, looked like a greyhound but ran and jumped like a small deer. It was a species not known to Banks. This was their first sighting of a kangaroo.

Days later a man reported seeing a slow-moving animal shaped like a small barrel and sporting two horns on its head. Banks later added wings to the description, said it was 'black as the devil',[41] and concluded that it was a large bat. Beaglehole suggests it was probably the Gould's Fruit-bat (*Pteropus gouldi*).[42] Two weeks later, while walking over the flats with his dogs, Banks came across four kangaroos, two of which his greyhound chased without success.

One day some Aboriginals visited their camp. Banks gave them some raw fish, but they gave it back to him, indicating they would like the fish to be cooked. When they were served the cooked fish, they ate only a small part of it, giving the rest to Banks's bitch, Lady.

Cook was delighted the relationship between his men and the indigenous people appeared to be improving. But this changed when Cook invited them on board *Endeavour*. When the Aboriginals saw some turtles on the deck, they tried to throw them over the side to where their canoes were tied. They were evicted from the ship. Banks, Cook and half a dozen others went across to the beach where there was a forge, a small fire with a pitch kettle boiling, a tent meant for Tupaia who was sick, and a sow with a

litter of young pigs. Further away the seine (fishing net) was spread out along the sand. One of the evicted Aboriginals approached the fire, lit a handful of dry grass and, before they realised what he was doing, made a large circuit of fire around them. The whole area went up in flames and one of the young pigs was scorched to death. Banks leapt into a boat to get help from men on *Endeavour*. Cook chased after the Aboriginals, but he had no gun, so when he saw them approach the seine with fire, he ran back to the beach to grab a musket. Cook fired at the group, who took off into the bush.

The Aboriginals later returned to the beach and peace was restored. But Cook did not trust them, and that night *Endeavour* was towed away from the beach in preparation for their departure. But the winds were unfavourable and they were stuck there.

Banks was desperate to get his hands on a kangaroo so he could examine it. Earlier that month Lieutenant Gore had shot a kangaroo but, rather than handing it over to Banks, he gave it to the cook and the men ate it. With *Endeavour* ready to sail, Banks took his dogs in search of the elusive animals. On 29 July he and his greyhound finally had some success. Coming across two adults and one very young kangaroo, the greyhound gave chase. While the older animals proved too nimble for him, the greyhound caught and killed the small kangaroo. At last, Banks had his specimen.

As they waited for the right breeze to take them out to the open sea, Parkinson made a list of the species of mammals he observed while they were in Australia. 'Of quadrupeds, there are goats, wolves, a small red animal about the size of a squirrel; a spotted one of the viverra kind, and an animal of a kind nearly approaching the mus genus (mouse), about the size of a greyhound.[43] As this was eighteen years before the First Fleet arrived in Australia, and the history books record the first goats introduced into Australia was via the First Fleet, Parkinson's report of observing goats on Australia's eastern coast in 1770 is surprising. It is doubtful that Parkinson would confuse the sighting of goats with another species of livestock. If he had seen goats, his observation suggests others had landed there earlier, or the goats had somehow 'drifted' from Indonesia.

Sailing Home

When out at sea it became evident that the crumbling *Endeavour* would not get them home. They made for the port of Batavia (Jakarta) so she could undergo repairs that were more extensive. After passing through what is now called Endeavour Strait (part of Torres Strait) into the Arafura Sea, on 3 September, Cook, Banks, Solander and some of Banks's servants landed at a small bay (Cook's Bay/Teluk Cook) on the west coast of New Guinea. They went in search of plants but were only there for two hours before they were attacked by some local people. The number grew to over a hundred frenzied locals. The Europeans quickly withdrew to their ship.

Their next port of call was at the small Indonesian island of Savu, where they hoped to find fresh meat. The Dutch had only recently settled Savu, and the sole Dutch agent was not keen to release livestock to the English. Ignoring the agent, Cook invited the King of Savu on board *Endeavour*. Seeing the animals on the top deck, the king expressed a desire for Cook's remaining English sheep. When Cook handed the sheep over, the king asked for one of Banks's dogs. A very reluctant Banks presented the king with his greyhound. In return for the dog they were permitted to purchase three hogs, thirty dozen fowl and a large quantity of eggs and coconuts, as well as six of the local sheep. According to Banks, the sheep were similar to the English Bengal breed, but instead of wool they had hair. Their noses were arched and their ears, hanging under their horns, were large and straight. Banks referred to them as 'Cabritos' and said they were easily confused with goats, given their resemblance to them. They also bought nine buffalo, slaughtering one bull weighing 360 pounds (about 163 kilograms) the following day.

With plenty of livestock on board, *Endeavour* sailed for Batavia. Cook knew Batavia was an unhealthy port, overcrowded with open, stinking drains and harbouring disease. Nevertheless, the dilapidated state of *Endeavour* left him with little choice. Three weeks later, on 11 October 1770, they anchored at the port of Batavia. Cook immediately began negotiations with the Dutch authorities to repair and supply *Endeavour*. The gentlemen took accommodation in the town and invited Tupaia, who had been ill for some weeks, to join them. Cook, his officers and the majority of the crew stayed on board *Endeavour*.

At Batavia, animals were plentiful. There were horses, cattle, buffalo, sheep, goats and hogs, the latter being of Chinese and European breeds. Parkinson described the Chinese pigs as being 'very fat, eat very well, and are cheap; but the Europeans despise them, and prefer the latter [the European breed], which are very dear.'[44] Banks also remarked on the Chinese pigs, saying they 'are so immensely fat that no one thinks of Buying the fat with the Lean; the Butcher when you buy it cuts off as much as you please and sells it to his countrymen the Chinese, who melt it down and eat it instead of Butter with their rice.'[45] Monkeys, considered a delicacy, were also available for consumption. Cook, Solander and Banks had never eaten monkey flesh, so decided to try it. On seeing the pitiful creatures in the market, chattering, their arms tied to some sticks and lying on their backs waiting to be killed, an empathetic Banks cut the strings that were tying the monkeys down and they immediately scampered off.

While they waited for the repairs to *Endeavour* to be completed, malaria and dysentery struck the ship's company. On 5 November the surgeon, William Monkhouse, was the first to die, followed closely by Tayeto then Tupaia. Seven of Cook's men died while they were anchored in Batavia, but more deaths would soon follow. Cook had to get his men out of the cesspool that was Batavia. But *Endeavour*'s bottom was in such a state that she was no longer able to return to sea. Worms had eaten away at her timbers, much of her sheathing was torn away, and there were planks missing. With most of his men sick, in desperation Cook employed most of the carpenters on shore to patch *Endeavour* and employed slaves to bail out the water that was in the hold. While the repairs were being actioned, Cook brought all his men onto the ship. But it was too late. Another twenty-two men would die before *Endeavour* anchored off the Cape of Good Hope. On

6 February 1771, Jonathan Monkhouse, the surgeon's brother who had saved *Endeavour* from sinking off the coral reef, died. The rest of the ship's company, including Cook, arrived at Table Bay, weak and defeated.

AT THE CAPE OF GOOD HOPE

As they recuperated under the African sun, Banks and Cook had time to study the diversity of Cape Town's livestock. The cattle and horses were smaller than English breeds. There was an abundance of sheep, goats and pigs and exotic animals. Banks made detailed notes on what was available (and these notes helped identify some of the species and breeds that Cook picked up in Cape Town on his subsequent voyages): 'The cattle are lighter than ours, more neatly made, and have horns that spread to a much wider extent. The sheep are clothed with a substance between wool and hair, and have tails of an enormous size. The horses, which were brought originally from Persia, are of a bay or chestnut colour, and rather small.' The dogs, however, he thought 'unsightly' and of little use. The goats were of various species. 'One, called the blue goat, is of a fine azure colour. The spotted goat is larger and beautifully marked with brown, white and red spots. The horns are a foot long. The rock-goat is no larger than a kid. The diving goat is much like the tame one, and receives its name from its method of squatting down in the grass to hide itself. We saw another animal called a goat, without any additional appellation, it is of the size of a hare, [a mature stag] and extremely beautiful … Amongst the hogs is the wild boar that is very fierce; and the earth hog which is of a red colour, and without teeth.'[46]

On 16 April 1771, surrounded by albatrosses and other seabirds, a travel-weary *Endeavour* sluggishly crept out of Table Bay. Perhaps Banks was no longer starving, or perhaps he joined the old mariners in their superstitions, because he did not kill any more albatrosses on this voyage. They stopped briefly at St Helena and then continued the slow journey towards home. Just a week out from England, Banks recorded the death of his remaining dog. Banks had rarely written more than a few lines in his diary each day since leaving St Helena on 4 May. He even omitted mentioning the death of Lieutenant Hicks, who finally succumbed to tuberculosis on 26 May. But five weeks later, on 1 July 1771, Banks recorded the death of his dog. Veiled beneath the detail is a deep attachment, suggesting Banks loved the dog that had almost completed a voyage around the world: 'My Bitch Lady was found dead in my Cabbin laying upon a stool on which she generally slept. She had been remarkably well for some days; in the night she shreikd out very loud so that we who slept in the great Cabbin heard her, but becoming quiet immediately no one regarded it. Whatever disease was the cause of her death it was the most sudden that ever came under my Observation.'

BANKS'S DOGS

It has long been presumed that Banks's bitch, Lady, was a greyhound, but there is no evidence to support this. Nowhere throughout Banks's notes, diaries or journals does he refer to his greyhound in either the plural or the feminine. Nor is there reference to two greyhounds, the greyhound's name or Lady's breed in any of the original manuscripts. Throughout the post-voyage literature, there is confusion around Lady's breed. She has been described as being 'a nondescript bitch'[47] and a spaniel.[48] One author describes Banks's dogs as 'hunting dogs and sporting dogs'[49] but later refers to them as 'Banks's greyhounds'. The bestselling author and journalist Rob Mundle suggests the bitch 'Lady' was Banks's greyhound and the dog was a spaniel.[50] An article, published in *New Zealand Geographic*, states the dogs were a greyhound and a spaniel: 'From Revesby, Banks's Lincolnshire estate, came two young African servants and his best dogs — a spaniel and a greyhound.'[51] Still another researcher wrote that when he took a passage on board the replica of *Endeavour*, he was given Banks's small cabin: 'a small

Banks's coffeepot, held at the Powerhouse Museum, Sydney. (Photo by author)

space that I later discovered was occupied not by Sir Joseph himself but by his dogs — a bitch spaniel called Lady used as gun dog, and a greyhound taken on board to run down game.'[52]

Circumstantial evidence suggests that Lady was likely to have been, if not a spaniel, then certainly a breed of water dog. Because she slept on a stool throughout the voyage in Banks's cramped, tiny cabin, it is probable she was a small breed, such as the now-extinct small English water spaniel. Further hints to Lady's breed come with the recommendations given to Joseph Banks by his close friend and esteemed naturalist, Thomas Pennant. On hearing Banks was about to embark on such a long and dangerous voyage, Pennant recommended a good water dog or two, 'also a fleet dog to pull down the guanacos.'[53] Why, if his knowledgeable and influential

friend recommended a water dog and a fleet dog (that is, a fast hunting dog) would Banks ignore his advice and take two greyhounds? The only explanation would be that Banks had a close affinity to two dogs of this breed, and yet there is no evidence that Banks had favourite pet dogs. In his early twenties, Banks was more a socialite than a man attached to animals.[54] There are no known personal paintings of him as a young man with a trusty hound, and no family portraits with a dog lingering in the background, with one exception — an illustration on a creamware coffee pot displayed at the Powerhouse Museum in Sydney.

The coffee pot was brought to the attention of the Captain Cook Society by Tony Norris and, dated 1770, it is believed to be authentic. On one side it portrays Banks having tea with his sister, Sarah

From Anderson's: A New, authentic, and complete collection of voyages round the world . . . published for Alex. Hogg, London 1784: 155

From Anderson's: A New, authentic, and complete collection of voyages round the world . . . published for Alex. Hogg, London 1784: 155

Banks. To the right and behind Banks is a black servant. Sitting on the ground, to the left of Sarah, is what looks like a small King Charles spaniel.

That Banks owned the two dogs is not in dispute. Based on Pennant's advice, it is reasonable to presume Banks purchased the two dogs specifically for the voyage. It is likely Banks included the two black men, who were supposedly 'house servants from his house in Chelsea, London'[55] but were actually retainers hired in London,[56] to care for the dogs. Both men had probably been slaves as 'the names of Banks's black servants was bestowed by him',[57] who became free men. Elizabeth Holmes refers to George Dorlton 'as a child of Jamaica … hired by Banks.'[58] James Roberts and Peter Briscoe (Banks's assistants who reputedly kept the most comprehensive list of those on board *Endeavour*) listed Dorlton as George Reepee,[59] which may have been his original name.

Also circumstantial, but nevertheless intriguing, is a sketch of Banks receiving a visit from the 'King of the Duke of York Island' (Mo'orea), Tahiti, on 3 June 1769.

In the centre of the picture is a pig and behind the pig is the silhouette of a dog that has no resemblance to a Tahitian dog or a greyhound. This particular image was published in Anderson's account[60] and was drawn retrospectively by a contemporary London artist who was not on the voyage and was sketching to instruction.[61] His illustration, created and published during Banks's lifetime (Joseph Banks died in 1820), suggests a water dog — possibly a spaniel or retriever — was present on the *Endeavour* voyage.

Added to these suppositions is the oil painting by the popular and successful portrait artist of the time, John Mortimer.

This painting was presumably commissioned by Lord Sandwich (Earl of Sandwich and First Lord of the Admiralty, John Montagu) to portray him with those who played a key role on the *Endeavour* voyage. In order from left to right are supposedly: Daniel Solander, Joseph Banks (sitting), James Cook, John Hawkesworth (commissioned by the Admiralty to write the official account of the voyage) and John Montagu. Lying in the foreground are two dogs. The dog on the right is clearly a small white and brown spaniel, very similar to a small English water spaniel. The other dog, sitting at the feet of Banks, is the size and colour of a greyhound, albeit a very well fed one. However, recent research has proven that the central figure, allegedly a young version of James Cook, is in fact Constantine Phipps[62] (an aristocrat, fellow botanist and long-time friend of Joseph Banks). Given the confusion around the human subjects in the painting, it is possible that Joseph Banks had Mortimer immortalise the dogs that accompanied him on this epic voyage.

Home

Nicholas Young, who was probably around fourteen years old by now, was first to glimpse home. As *Endeavour* limped into the Downs on Saturday, 13 July 1771, the only remaining livestock on board were a few ailing sheep Cook had purchased at Cape Town, and the robust little English milch goat, the first female of any species to survive two circumnavigations of the world.

When Joseph Banks stepped off *Endeavour*, he stepped into glory. The newspapers loved him and he was celebrated across England. Banks and Dr Solander, accompanied by the President of the Royal Society, were presented to King George III. A jubilant Banks gave the king a coronet of gold set with feathers collected on the voyage.

When Cook stepped off *Endeavour*, he stepped into a period of grief. But first, he had one final instruction to follow. Cook called into the Admiralty Office and provided a full account of the voyage. Once this duty was complete, Cook went home to his family. Reunited with his wife, Elizabeth, he was free to grieve for two of his children. His only daughter, four-year-old Elizabeth, died three months before *Endeavour*'s return. Baby Joseph, whom Cook had never met, died at the age of four months, in October 1772. Cook did not go home alone, as the goat from *Endeavour* was with him. She was to be a pet for Cook's surviving sons, seven-year-old James and six-year-old Nathaniel.

Endeavour's Goat

Goat's story did not end with *Endeavour*'s return to England. While it was widely believed that Joseph Banks was her owner, she ended her days in the Cook family's small backyard in Mile End Road. 'And many were those who came to see her, as did Sir Joseph Banks and even Lord Sandwich who stood, as he said, hat in hand "To pay his respects".[63] Having survived two circumnavigations, Goat attracted some attention. In several British newspapers an article on the *Endeavour* voyage ended with the paragraph: 'Before I conclude, I must not omit how highly we have been indebted to a milch goat: she was three years in the West Indies, and was once round the world before in the *Dolphin*, and never went dry the whole time; we mean to reward her services in a good English pasture for life.'[64]

Sketch modelled on a photograph by Lou Alexander: Arapawa doe 'Kiwi' and kid 'Coffee Bean' from Sedgwick County Zoo, USA. Artist: Lex McKay © 2019

Goat's fame spread beyond England. On 16 February 1773 a gentleman living in Egypt wrote to his London physician, asking him to pass on his compliments to the *Endeavour*'s goat and to say that he was envious of her having sailed around the world on several occasions.[65] Impressed with Goat on the long, hazardous sea voyage, Banks and Solander requested the famous lexicographer, Dr Samuel Johnson, write a motto to be inscribed on a silver collar they purchased for her. The following day Johnson sent Joseph Banks the following epigram:

Perpetui ambita bis terra praemia lactis,
Haec habet altrici Capra secunda Jovis.

This was translated and expanded to:

In fame scarce second to the nurse of Jove, This Goat, who twice the world has traversed round,
Deserving both her master's care and love,
Ease and perpetual pasture now has found.[66]

Goat never returned to sea. There was a rumour the British Government of the time discussed granting her a pension and admitting her to the privileges of Greenwich Park, the Royal Navy's homes for sailors where James Cook had rooms. But there is no evidence of this and Goat did not live long enough to enjoy the pension or to forage in the park's gardens. She died on 28 March 1772. Cook must have felt a great attachment to this long-serving goat, for he noted the date in his personal diary, usually reserved for private matters to share with his wife.

GOAT'S MILK

Endeavour's nanny goat was more than just a loved pet and utility animal. Through her milk she may have contributed to the success of Cook's voyages to the Southern Ocean. While the men showed symptoms of scurvy, not one man who sailed on *Endeavour* died directly from the dreaded disease. There is no doubt Cook's approach to the men's hygiene and diet were significant factors in preventing scurvy. Cook knew vitamin C was a key preventative against scurvy and that is why he insisted the men eat sauerkraut and drink lemon juice. What Cook would not have known is that goats' milk is high in vitamins A and B, and has traces of vitamins C, D, E and K. Nor would he have realised that the vitamin content of sauerkraut is reduced when it is boiled. And while lemons are high in vitamin C, Cook's preserved 'lemon' was not made with lemons at all, but with West Indian limes which contain almost no vitamin C.[67]

Goat, on the other hand, never ran dry and her milk was always fresh. When the men were sick and unable to eat, they were given sips of her lifesaving, vitamin-rich milk.

BETWEEN THE FIRST AND SECOND VOYAGES

While most of the glory of the *Endeavour* expedition went to Banks and Solander, after completing the necessary documentation and reporting to the Admiralty, James Cook received recognition for a successful voyage by being promoted to Captain. Cook and Banks developed a mutual respect, almost a friendship, during the voyage. Cook would first learn of his promotion through Banks, who was a close friend of the first Lord of the Admiralty, Lord Sandwich. With the promotion came a new command that would keep Cook in London, preparing his charts and journals for publication. As Cook wrote factual reports, sketched detailed maps and requested promotions and commissions for the men who had sailed with him, Banks was busily avoiding a woman he had proposed to in 1768, and preparing details on 17,000 plant specimens he had collected throughout the voyage.

Speculation began that there was to be another expedition, with Banks pursuing further discoveries in the Southern Ocean. On Banks's recommendation, James Cook was summoned to an interview with King George III, where he was invited to explain his charts and receive his commission as a commander.

There was to be a second voyage. Not only was the Great Southern Continent still to be discovered, Cook was 'to convey the conveniences of life, as fowls, dogs, goats, cattle, corn, iron, etc., to those remote regions which were destitute of them.'[68] Cook recommended this next voyage be timed to coincide with the southern hemisphere's summer months, and that they proceed eastwards via the Cape of Good Hope. This new route would enable him to purchase stock relatively cheaply from Cape Town. It also offered the animals meant for the South Pacific islands a greater chance of surviving the voyage. Knowing the perils they faced, Cook suggested a second ship accompany them.

The new voyage was due to commence in March 1772, but it was delayed due to the ships not being ready. James Cook would be home when the goat from the *Endeavour* voyage died. No one knew what the problem was but Cook had an idea. He wrote, 'She is a sea-goat, she fretted for the ocean. Our back garden, with plenty of land and the attention of all of London, is not what nourished her.'[69]

While the British were planning their next expedition to the South Pacific, two French ships — the *Mascarin* and *Marquis de Castries* — under the command of Marion du Fresne, were sailing towards the South Indian Ocean.

Marion du Fresne

Marion d*u Fresne's expedition* was the second by the French to visit New Zealand, following that of de Surville in December 1769. Du Fresne was a wealthy French naval commander who, like Cook, embarked on a voyage of discovery in search of the Great Southern Continent. After stopping at the Cape of Good Hope for provisions, including sheep, kids and pigs, du Fresne proceeded to Tasmania. There he came into conflict with some Aboriginals and decided to steer for New Zealand. On 25 March 1772, they sighted Mount Egmont but did not land. Sailing to the north, the French moored at Spirits Bay (Kapowairua) at the very north of the country where some of the men happened upon 'a skeleton of an ass of the same kind as ours.'[70] Alongside the skeleton was what they perceived to be the skin of a bear. Returning to their ships, they rounded North Cape and continued southward, anchoring in the Bay of Islands on 11 May.

Receiving a warm welcome from Māori, the French crews stayed there for five weeks. They established a camp for their sick, many of whom suffered from scurvy. While their crew slowly recovered, the French explored the area, cut down trees to repair the ships, and befriended and traded with local Māori. The only live animals they recorded observing on land were dogs and rats. The latter, according to Julien Crozet, Second Lieutenant on *Mascarin*, were similar to those that lurked in the French fields and forests. Māori dogs, he said, were plentiful and resembled a domestic fox: 'quite black or white, very low on the legs, straight ears, thick tail, long body, full jaws but more pointed than that of the fox, and uttering the same cry; they do not bark like our dogs.'[71] The French took some of the dogs on board to be pets, but found they were unable to tame them. It was a period of sharing, healing, trade and friendship. However, something changed. On 11 June, several Māori visited the camp established by the French for the ailing sailors. Showing interest in the tents and the guns, the chief invited Lieutenant Jean Roux to visit their village. Roux called in later that afternoon and became suspicious when the chief asked a lot of questions about cleaning and firing the guns. Deciding to demonstrate the guns' ability to kill, Roux shot a dog that was walking past. He then handed the chief the gun, and he too aimed at a nearby dog. But instead of pulling the trigger, the chief blew on the lock. Rather than demonstrating how to fire the musket correctly, Roux cautiously left the village and reported his concerns to du Fresne. Du Fresne shrugged off the warning.

At the invitation of two chiefs who had befriend him, du Fresne, accompanied by two armed men and thirteen sailors, went to their village. Shortly after they arrived at the village, the French party were killed. Unaware of the fate of their comrades, the following day a second group of French went ashore to their death. Twenty-five Frenchmen died, but one seaman escaped to warn the others. Violent reprisals by the remaining French caused an estimated 250 Māori deaths. Following the slaughter, the French left New Zealand, sailing for the central Pacific and on to the Philippines.

Lieutenant Roux was one of the French survivors. In his memoirs he provides more information on the death of du Fresne and his men. However, it is the story of the animals that are the focus of this book, and as none were involved in the massacre, we can focus on the skeleton of the large animal they found in Spirits Bay. Roux claimed the skeleton was an ass similar to those commonly found in France during the late eighteenth century. Given the earlier voyagers' observations, it is hard to imagine any animal existing in New Zealand during this period that remotely resembled an ass. We know Cook did not carry an ass on board *Endeavour*. The most probable explanation for the skeleton is that de Surville, on *St Jean Baptiste*, brought the ass to New Zealand. How it came to be in Spirits Bay is unclear. It is possible the ass died on board ship, the carcass was thrown into the sea and washed ashore with the tide. The ass may have wandered over time from another anchorage, or perhaps de Surville landed there, although this was never recorded.

This is not the first time an animal, believed to be an ass, was seen in the South Pacific. On 24 January 1767, while in the Straits of Magellan, Wallis from *Dolphin* reported sighting an animal resembling an ass 'but it had a cloven hoof … and was as swift as a deer.'[72] It is probable that what Wallis saw was a guanaco (a camelid, similar to a llama), common to South America. Whether the skeleton on New Zealand's beach was an ass, a guanaco or belonged to some other large animal, there is no recorded explanation as to how it happened to be on the northern tip of New Zealand's North Island.

Endnotes

1   J. Banks. & J.D. Hooker (Ed.). (1896). *Journal of the Right Hon. Sir Joseph Banks during Captain Cook's first voyage in H.M.S. Endeavour in 1768–71 to Terra del Fuego, Otahite, New Zealand, Australia, the Dutch East Indies, etc.* London: MacMillan & Co.

2   Ibid.

3   J. Bootie (1768–1771). *A journal of the proceedings of his Majesty's Bark* Endeavour. *Commencing from 27th May 1768 to the 24th Nov 1769.* Ref. 51/4546. Sydney: Mitchell Library Museum.

4   A. Villiers (1967). *Captain Cook, the seamen's seaman.* UK. London: Hodder & Stoughton: 86.

5   R.W. Stevens (1858). *On the Stowage of Ships and their Cargoes.* London: Stevens; Plymouth: Longmans: 157.

6   Sparrman 1953: 42

7   R. Hough (1994). *Captain James Cook: a biography.* London: Hodder & Stoughton: 76

8   Ibid.

9   Banks & Hooker 1896.

10   F. McLynn (2011). *Captain Cook: master of the seas.* London: Yale University Press: 85.

11   H.G. Beulah & E.G. Hancock (2018). 'The 'Lost' Types of Carabus Pallens Fabricius, 1775 (Coleoptera: Carabidae: Lebiinae) from the Banks and Hunter Collections: Lectotype Designation, Redescription, and Distribution', *The Coleopterists Bulletin* 72: 4, pp. 845–57.

12   J.C. Beaglehole (Ed.). (1962). *The* Endeavour *Journal of Joseph Banks 1768– 1771.* (Vols. 1 & 2). Australia: Angus and Robertson: 59.

13   Banks & Hooker 1896: 136.

14   Hough 1994: 114.

15   M. Sahlins (1995). *How 'Natives' think: about Captain Cook, for example.* Chicago: University of Chicago Press: 160–61.

16   C.H. Smith (1840). *The Natural History of Dogs: canidae or genus canis of authors; including also the genera hyaena and proteles.* Vol. 2. Edinburgh: 211.

17   C. Catton (1788). *Animals, drawn from nature and engraved in aqua-tinta.* London: I & J Taylor: 41.

18   Banks journal: 23 September 1769.

19   S. Parkinson & W. Kenrick (1773). *A journal of a voyage to the South Seas in his Majesty's ship, the Endeavour. Faithfully transcribed from the papers of the late Sydney Parkinson. Draughtsman to Joseph Banks, Esq., on his late expedition with Dr. Solander, round the world.* London: Printed for Stanfield Parkinson: 89.

20   Ibid: 99.

21   A. Salmond (2003). *The Trial of the Cannibal Dog: Captain Cook in the South Seas.* London: Allen Lane for the Penguin Press.

22   Banks: 21 October 1769.

23   M. Appleton (1958). *They Came to New Zealand: an account of New Zealand from the earliest times up to the middle of the nineteenth century.* London: Methuen & Co. Ltd: 40.

24   https://teara.govt.nz/en/biographies/1c23/colenso-william

25   W. Colenso (1877, 8 October). *Notes, chiefly historical, on the ancient Dog of the New Zealanders.* Read before the Hawke's Bay Philosophical Institute. Christchurch: Kiwi Publishers, Retrieved: 2018 (NZ Electronic Text Collection: http://nzetc.victoria.ac.nz/tm/scholarly/tei-NZETC).

26   The Hunterian Museum in Glasgow holds a collection of Māori cloaks authenticated as dating back to the eighteenth century and presumed collected during Cook's voyages.

27   E.W. Mackie (1985). *William Hunter and Captain Cook: the Eighteenth Century ethnographical collection in the Hunterian Museum.* Glasgow: 9.

28   K.A. Wodzicki (1950). *Introduced mammals of New Zealand. An ecological and economic survey.* Wellington. Department of Scientific & Industrial Research Bulletin No. 98: 88.

29   G.M. Thomson (1921). *Wildlife in New Zealand. Part I.—Mammalia.* Wellington: Government Printer: 84.

30   W. Vance (1976): *Bush, bullocks, and boulders.* The Alford Forest Bushside Springburn District Centenary Committee: 10.

31   D.M. Cunningham & P.J. Moors (1996). *Guide to the Identification and Collection of New Zealand Rodents.* (3rd ed.). Wellington: Department of Conservation: 10–11.

32   A. Salmond (1991). *Two Worlds: first meetings between Māori and Europeans 1642–1772.* Honolulu: University of Hawaii Press: 181–82.

33   C.O. Davis (1876). *The Life and Times of Patuone, the Celebrated Ngapuhi Chief.* J.H. Field, Albert Street, Auckland: Steam Printing Office: 7.

34   Ibid.

35   J. Dunmore (1969). *The Fateful Voyage of the* St Jean Baptiste: *a true account of M. de Surville's expedition to New Zealand & the unknown South Seas in the Years 1769–70.* Christchurch: Pegasus Press: 82.

36   Banks journal, 15 January 1770.

37   Beaglehole 1961: 286

38   Parkinson 1773: 122.

39   G. Edwards (1858). *Gleanings of natural history, exhibiting figures of quadrupeds, birds,*

insects, plants etc. with … descriptions of seventy different subjects, designed, engraved and coloured after nature, on fifty copper-plate prints. London: Printed for the author, at the Royal College of Physicians, in Warwick Lane: 126.

40 Kippis 1788: 152

41 Banks in Hooker, 1896: 282.

42 Beaglehole 1967: 352.

43 Parkinson 1773: 145.

44 Ibid: 180.

45 J.C. Beaglehole (Ed.). (1962). *The* Endeavour *Journal of Joseph Banks 1768–1771.* (Vols. 1 & 2). Australia: Angus and Robertson: 204.

46 G.W. Anderson (1784). *A new, authentic, and complete collection of voyages round the world, undertaken and performed by royal authority: containing an authentic, entertaining, full, and complete history of Captain Cook's first, second, third and last voyages, undertaken by order of his present Majesty, for making discoveries in geography, navigation, astronomy, &c. in the southern and northern hemispheres &c.* London. Printed for Alex. Hogg: 94.

47 P. O'Brian (1987). *Joseph Banks: a life.* Chicago: University of Chicago Press: 76.

48 A. Macarthur (1997). *His Majesty's Bark* Endeavour: *the story of the ship and her people.* Australia: Angus & Robertson: 13.

49 P. Aughton (1999). Endeavour: *the story of Captain Cook's first great epic voyage.* Great Britain: The Windrush Press: 15.

50 Mundle 2013: 108.

51 R. Hunt (2010). 'Joseph Banks', *New Zealand Geographic*, 101: Jan–Feb.

52 M. Moran (2003). *Beyond the Coral Sea: travels in the old empires of the South West Pacific.* London: Harper Collins Publishers.

53 T. Pennant & Banks, J. (1767). *Correspondence between Thomas Pennant (22 letters) and Joseph Banks (3 Letters).* Retrieved May 1, 2018. (books.google.co.nz/books/about/).

54 Private correspondence with Christine Chapman of the Sir Joseph Banks Society.

55 R. Bloomfield (2013) *Wake of the Endeavour: New Revised Edition.* Amazon Kindle Books.

56 McLynn 2011: 87.

57 Aughton 1999: 15.

58 E. Holmes (2017). 'Joseph Banks, botanist and patron, and: not recorded: Dorlton and Richmond, servants, and: not recorded: Girl', *Southern Review*, 53: 4, pp. 478–82. Project MUSE, muse.jhu.edu/article/663673: 480.

59   J. Roberts (1771). *A journal of His Majesty's bark* Endeavour *round the world, Lieut. James Cook, Commander, 27th May 1768', 27 May – 14 May 1770, with annotations.* Mitchell Library, Australia: 2; Briscoe, P. (1771). *A journal of His Majesty's Bark* Endeavour *by God's permission bound to the South Seas, Lieutenant James Cook, Commander, 27th May 1768–14 May 1770.* SAFE/DLMS 96. State Library of New South Wales Collection: 4

60   Anderson 1784: 15.

61   National Library of New Zealand.

62   Cook's Log, July 2009: 37

63   J. Dunmore (2006). *Mrs Cook's Book of Recipes for Mariners in Distant Seas.* Sydney: Australian National Maritime Museum: 32–33.

64   J.C. Beaglehole (1955). *The Life of Captain James Cook: The voyage of the* Endeavour, *1768–1771.* Cambridge University Press: 649.

65   E.W. Montague (1773). Published in the Sentimental & Masonic Magazine for July 1792, Dublin.

66   J. Boswell (1822). *The life of Samuel Johnson, L.L.D: Comprehending an account of his studies and numerous works in chronological order, a series of his epistolary correspondence and conversations with many eminent persons, and various original pieces of his composition, never before published ...* In two volumes. London: 134.

67   I. Cameron (1987). *Lost Paradise: the exploration of the Pacific.* London: Century: 115.

68   R. Sherrin & J. Wallace (1890). *Early history of New Zealand Brett's historical series, from earliest times to 1840, by R.A.A. Sherrin. From 1840 to 1845, by J. H. Wallace.* In T.W. Leys (Ed.). Auckland: H Brett: 39.

69   M. Day (2002). *Mrs Cook: the real and imagined life of the Captain's wife.* Australia: Allen & Unwin: 199.

70   McNab 1914b: 61

71   J.M. Crozet (1891). *Crozet's voyage to Tasmania, New Zealand and the Ladrone Islands and the Philippines in the years 1771–1771.* Translated by A. Rochon. Cambridge: Cambridge University Press: 76.

72   G. Robertson & H. Carrington (1948). *The discovery of Tahiti. A journal of the second voyage of H.M.S.* Dolphin *round the world, under the command of Captain Wallis, R.N. in the years 1766, 1767 and 1768.* London: The Hakluyt Society: 55.

Cook's Second Voyage Around the World

COOK'S SECOND VOYAGE IN *RESOLUTION*, ACCOMPANIED BY *ADVENTURE*

Chapter 3

PREPARING FOR THE VOYAGE

The wealthy Joseph Banks liked the idea of another journey to the South Pacific, but this time on a much grander scale than the *Endeavour* voyage. Banks also fancied himself as commander of the voyage, but he was a civilian, not a seaman. He made a few recommendations to his friend, Lord Sandwich, First Lord of the Admiralty. Subsequently, the post went to newly promoted Captain James Cook.

Cook's primary orders were to determine if the Great Southern Continent existed. If it did exist, he was to claim it for England. The route he was to take was via Cape Town. There he would purchase animals as gifts for the people living in the Pacific. First, Cook was to sail from Africa to the south, going as close to the South Pole as was humanly possible.

Endeavour was unfit for a second voyage around the world and was refitted then sold as a collier ship. Cook went in search of another ship that would cope with the rigours of sailing into Antarctic waters. He selected the relatively new *Marquis of Granby* (she was only fourteen months old) for himself, renaming her *Resolution*. She was over 110 feet long and had a larger hold than *Endeavour*. Cook selected the *Marquis of Rockingham* as his support ship and renamed her *Adventure*. This ship would be under the command of Tobias Furneaux, a popular and experienced seaman who had sailed with Wallis in *Dolphin*.

As Cook prepared for the voyage ahead, Banks was making his own arrangements. He selected sixteen support staff that included two musicians to entertain him on the voyage. To accommodate his entourage, Banks paid for some extensive alterations to *Resolution*, including a new top deck. *Resolution* consequently became top heavy and unseaworthy and at Cook's request the Royal Navy demolished Banks's additions. Banks threw a tantrum, swearing and stamping his feet on the wharf, finally removing himself and his retinue from the voyage. No doubt pleased to be back in control of the expedition, Cook looked for their replacements. The navy employed two German naturalists, John Reinhold (Johann) Forster and his son, seventeen-year-old Georg Forster, to replace Banks and Solander.

THE SHIPS' COMPANIES

One hundred and twelve men left England on *Resolution*, twenty of whom had earlier sailed with Cook on *Endeavour*. These

By NZ portrait artist, Alan Sanders ©2018. (Permission granted). It is based on the famous Nathaniel Dance portrait which shows Cook in his Captain's Dress uniform. Dance's portrait is considered by some to be the best likeness of Cook.

included Richard Pickersgill, now a Third Lieutenant; Charles Clerke promoted to Second Lieutenant; and John Edgcumbe, now Lieutenant of Marines. The Master on *Resolution* was Joseph Gilbert, older than most of the men at forty. Perhaps it was because Gilbert was also a draughtsman that he and Cook got on well together. Also on *Resolution* was a very experienced seaman, James Burney, whose father was a friend of Lord Sandwich.

Adventure had a complement of eighty-one. Joseph Shanks was First Lieutenant, Arthur Kempe was Second Lieutenant, and her Master was Peter Fannin, a talented chart-maker. Both ships had a contingent of marines and both had an astronomer. William Wales was the astronomer on *Resolution* and William Bayly was the astronomer on *Adventure*. Accommodated on *Resolution* was William Hodges, the artist employed to sketch people and landscapes discovered on the voyage.

With the lower decks crammed with stores to last at least two and a half years, livestock were loaded onto the top deck of both vessels. These included sheep, goats, hogs and poultry, including geese, and a couple of small bullocks. Poultry, goats and pigs would prove to be ideal livestock for long sea voyages. Poultry provided a regular supply of eggs, goats gave fresh milk and the pigs, with their gestation period of only three months, provided a regular supply of fresh meat. The large English breed of pigs were particularly desirable. They were easily penned, could survive on food scraps, had large litters and the piglets grew quickly.

Once the animals were in their cages and stalls, the crew received an advancement of their pay. To prevent them from deserting, the masters confined the men to their respective ships and handed out free grog. A few hours into their revelry, Johann and Georg Forster, the new appointed naturalists, joined *Resolution*.

Johann began his journal in the same manner that he would follow throughout the voyage, with a grumble: 'I came on board but the ship was all in a confusion, and I could range nothing in my and my son's cabbin.' [1] Their berths cluttered, the crew too drunk to help them, the disgruntled Forsters left the ship and stayed in the town overnight. They returned to the ship intending to organise their cabin, but it was still a mess. Johann complained to the Master, who offered him alternative accommodation. Descending a ladder to a space as dark as a dungeon below the waterline, Forster's nose was attacked by an intolerable thick stench of decaying matter. The Master's Mate came behind him, holding up a dim light. Forster followed the mate to a series of boxed spaces, one on top of another, each less than six feet wide and about six feet deep. Secured at the entrance of each bunk was a piece of canvas, meant to provide some protection from the cold and to allow privacy for the occupant. This was accommodation reserved for lesser officers on the sailing ships. Ordinary seamen simply slung their hammocks close together in spaces relative to their status. Forster opted to endure the inconvenience of the cramped cabin allocated to them, but it was too late. The Master had already found another use for it. Forster checked it out. 'The room offered me by Captain Cook, and which the Master's obstinacy deprived me of, was now given to very peaceably bleating creatures,

who on a stage raised up as high as my bed,
shit and pissed on one side, whilst five goats
did the same afore on the other side.'[2]

Gilbert put them into a smaller cabin
nestled between two large guns. As paid
employees of the Royal Navy, the naturalists
did not have the option of slinging their
hammocks in the Great Cabin. Cook must
have been so relieved.

Chapter 4

COOK'S SECOND CIRCUMNAVIGATION

Early on the morning of 13 July 1772, *Resolution* and *Adventure* prepared to slip out of Plymouth Sound. A now-famous painting depicts the scene. Hammond, a London ship owner, commissioned Francis Holman to paint *Resolution* and *Adventure* leaving England.

In all the paintings of *Resolution*, the figurehead on her bow is difficult to discern. Yet a decorative figurehead plays an important role as it advertises the name and role of the ship. A model of a sailing ship, mistakenly believed to be *Resolution*, had a figurehead of a native holding a spear and shield.[3] There

Thomas Luny sketch of Resolution's Figurehead. Title: 'Sketch of the stern of Resolution with notes'. Repro ID: PV9686-2. Photograph by Jan Nauta, 1991; supplied by John Allan

is a painting of *Resolution* by John Webber in the British Library with a label claiming the figurehead is a sea serpent. Experts at Wellington's Museum of New Zealand, Te Papa Tongarewa, believe it to be a hound in full cry. Recent evidence proves that the figurehead on *Resolution* was an animal. Held at London's National Maritime Museum is a pencil sketch by Thomas Luny, a student of Francis Holman, dated 1778. The figurehead illustrated and labelled 'Resolution' is a prancing horse under the bowsprit, its back legs either side of the bow.[4]

Today a prancing horse is one of the most recognised logos in the world and a symbol of high performance, such as Ferrari's prancing horse. How apt that Cook's second and third expeditions were steered by such an animal.

Cook began his second circumnavigation of the world 'accompanied by the sound of bellowing bullocks, grunting hogs, cackling fowls, guttural goats and bewildered sheep.'[5] Tracking the start of *Endeavour*'s route, their first stop would be Madeira.

Madeira to the Cape Verde Islands

On 29 July 1772, two weeks after leaving Plymouth, they arrived at Madeira. When the first gun fired to salute the castle, Johann Forster jumped out of bed, quickly dressed and departed before the guns on either side of the cabin let rip. He meandered on land and, having given himself the important portfolio of describing any animals they happened upon, noted oxen and cows, horses, mules, asses, goats, pigs, sheep, dogs and cats. He saw only one feral animal, the common grey rabbit. Three days later, loaded with wine, fruit, vegetables, fish and more livestock to replenish their food supplies, they left Madeira.

Following a south-west course, they crossed the Tropic of Cancer into an uncomfortable humidity. The moisture of the sea air, combined with the sweat and breath of the men and animals between decks, made everything damp. Despite the portholes being open, body odour permeated the lower decks, forcing the crew out of their mess into the fresh air. Anything made of leather, including the covers of books, developed a slimy fungus. Johann Forster complained, but Cook had greater concerns.

With the humidity came an increase in insect infestation. Newly hatched cockroaches were so thick in the hold, buckets could scoop them up. Cook gave the order to fumigate below to get rid of the noxious gases, the moisture and the vermin. He then ordered everyone to proceed to the top deck, bringing up any animals from below. Men closed the portholes and sealed loose boards and hatchways. Over one hundred men squeezed on the top deck with an array of animals. While most of the livestock was contained, the ship's cats and goats remained at liberty. Some of the crew created smoke by lighting a combination of charcoal and pitch, then piped it below. Hours passed as they waited for the fumigation process to be completed. Then there was a sudden explosion! On the top deck, casks full of beer and malt had been fermenting in the heat. One burst and liquor cascaded everywhere. Men and animals scrambled to collect the prized liquid, but the ship's goats got there first: 'Our goats were very active to profit by it and to lick up of the liquor so much, that they often were quite inebriated and lay panting and breathing on deck as if they were dying.'[6] The gases from the lower decks disappeared with the smoke, the insect population was temporarily controlled and the goats recovered. However, the uncomfortable heat continued and the nauseating smells returned.

Animals at St Jago

In the middle of August 1772, they reached the Cape Verde Islands off West Africa. Anchoring at Port Praya on the island of St Jago (Santiago), they went to purchase fresh food to continue their journey, but there was little surplus food available. French, Dutch, English and Portuguese ships, all carrying cargo to the East Indies, had arrived before them. The extreme scarcity of livestock and fresh produce made their stay at Port Praya very short. After only one full day in the harbour, they were obliged to content themselves with a few casks of brackish water, a single small bullock, a few long-legged goats and some wretched lean hogs, turkeys and chickens. The only fruits they could get were a few hundred unripe oranges and some dry bananas.

Having acquired what they could, Cook ordered everyone back to the ships. Crew transported the animals from the shore to the ship using the small boats. The surf was high and the animals terrified. The crew managed to get the goats, pigs, monkeys and chooks to the ships, but the bullock would not cooperate. The men dragged the reluctant animal into the sea with a thick rope wrapped around his horns and another rope tied around one of his hind legs. As they pulled him through the surf, the man who had the rope around the bullock's horns let it go, which left several men dragging it by the hind leg. The terrified beast panicked, and so did the men. They rushed back to the shore to get another rope, leaving the splashing creature to the mercy of the breakers. They returned to the drowning animal with another rope, managed to secure the new rope around its horns and very slowly towed the exhausted, unresisting bullock towards the ship. Suddenly, a rogue wave lifted them up, rolled the boat over and the men were thrown into the sea. They had worked too hard to get this animal to lose him now. Clinging tight to the ropes, the saturated men righted the boat, clambered in and dragged the bullock to the ship. Hauled on board barely alive, it was slaughtered a couple of days later.

From St Jago to Cape Town

Some of the men acquired a pet at St Jago. The island had monkeys that were not much bigger than cats. They were a greenish-brown colour with black faces and paws and a kind of pouch on each side of their mouth. Forster

said they most resembled a drawing of the pigmy ape by Thomas Pennant; the only difference was the St Jago monkey had a tail.

Pennant 1771, No. 95: 27

The sailors purchased about twenty of the monkeys, but it was not until they got them on board that they discovered the cute little animals were full of lice. The mischievous animals roamed freely around the ship, defecating at will. When the sailors eventually became bored with their pets, Cook ordered the monkeys thrown overboard. Revealed in this order, which is abhorrent to most of us, is the character of James Cook. He was a realist. The men were bored with the monkeys; therefore, the animals were no longer useful as pets. If the monkeys stayed on *Resolution*, they would get in the way of sailors and eat food needed for animals that were more productive. Cook was also a leader who made the hard calls when it was necessary. By ordering the men to throw their unwanted pets overboard, Cook took the responsibility away from them. He also demonstrated empathy towards the monkeys. Rather than a slow death by starvation, Cook gave them a quicker, less brutal end by drowning. Possibly, due to his experience with Banks and the monkeys at Batavia, this was one of the very rare occasions on the voyage when animals were disposed of and not consumed. For the health-conscious captain, it was the monkeys or his men. The monkeys were incubators for fleas and lice, their faeces carriers of bacteria.

Lieutenant John Elliott was fond of his pet and hid the monkey inside a coat. It escaped a couple of months later. John Whitehouse, the Master's Mate, was sitting in the officers' mess writing a letter. The monkey approached him and threw ink over the letter. A furious Whitehouse 'drew his pistol and blasted the monkey out the window'.[7] Elliott never forgave him, describing Whitehouse in his memoirs as a hypocritical, mischievous man.

A little swallow entertained the crew a few days later. It followed and circled the ship from noon until sunset, eventually settling on the side of the ship. Disturbed by the trimming of the sails, the bird flew to an inaccessible place on board where it could rest in peace. It flitted around the ship for days, resting on the quarter-galley or the carving at the stern. When a heavy shower of rain fell, the bird's plumage became saturated and, unable to fly, it settled on the railing of the quarterdeck. Georg Forster picked it up and dried it. When the swallow recovered, he released it in the lower deck amongst the cargo where it fed on flies. At dinnertime, the swallow flew through an open porthole, returning at dusk. The next morning it returned to the cargo deck and caught another feed of flies. For several days the swallow hovered around various parts of the ship, until one day, it disappeared. It was last seen flying around the cabin of the astronomer, William Wales. While not accusing Wales directly,

Georg Forster claimed some vile person had snatched his bird and fed it to one of the ship's cats. Johann Forster also believed one of the seamen had deliberately killed the bird:'His sudden disappearance made me apprehend the worst for his life; for we had some very cruel and ill-natured people in the Ship; who made it their business to disturb other peoples happiness and enjoyments; this prompted me to pay the tribute of a tear to the memory of my little friend.'[8]

With the crew unable to replenish their casks at St Jago, the stored drinking water turned into a putrid, stinking mess full of maggots and wriggling worms. To freshen the water, they transferred it into horse buckets, took it up onto the top deck then poured it down canvas hoses into empty containers in the hold. This process was repeated until the water was considered fit for drinking and then fed to the thirsty animals. For the men, there was distilling equipment on board both ships that converted seawater into relatively fresh water.

The closer they sailed to the equator, the hotter it became. On 9 September they crossed the line, going through the usual ritual of celebrating and dunking those on board that had never crossed the equator before. Unlike the first voyage, there is no mention of animals added to the blacklist on this journey.

Cape Town to the Antarctic Circle

Seen on the horizon towards the end of October was Cape Town's Table Mountain. *Adventure* was still some distance away, so Cook decided to wait for Furneaux so the ships could go into the Bay together. Darkness

Sparrman 1785: facing the title page. Accessed: the Alexander Turnbull Library, Rare Books & Fine Printing: qREng SPAR Voya 1785.

fell and the ocean took on the appearance of fire. Fascinated, Johann Forster lowered a bucket and scooped up a sample of the red seawater. He peered into the bucket and saw a mass of minuscule bodies racing around in the water. Forster put the bucket on the deck and left it to stand. Slowly the tiny animals disappeared and the water returned to a normal colour. When Forster dipped his finger into the bucket and stirred the contents, the animals reactivated and swum wildly in all directions. The water again glowed red. This was Forster's introduction to marine bioluminescence: living organisms in the water were creating light. Now joined by *Adventure*, the ships entered Table Bay.

When the men from *Resolution* stepped on shore, three St Jago monkeys were released into the countryside. Elliott was not the only one who had tried to save his pet.

They were at the Cape for three weeks, allowing time for repairs to be made to the ships, decks and hulls scrubbed, and the rigging reset. They purchased supplies, including brandy, livestock and other necessities. Four English sheep, all wethers (castrated rams), were traded for eight of the Cape's wethers, which were deemed to be of lesser quality. These were destined for the officers' table. Forster thought this a very bad bargain: 'English sheep had better coats, were more used to the cold climate, and to the sea, and had more flesh and fat upon them and might by a little feeding come so far as to weigh 80 lb a piece [about 36 kilograms]; whereas these poor Cape sheep hardly weigh half that weight.'[9] Cook bought two entire rams and four ewes for breeding stock. These were most probably of the common South African breed whose large tails consisted of pure fat.

The Forsters wanted a dog that would fetch game for them when they reached the Pacific Islands, and they set their hearts on a water spaniel. While terrier and the larger staghound breeds were common, water spaniels were scarce at Cape Town. Refusing to compromise, the Forsters searched the town for a water spaniel. Eventually they found a young male, but the owner would only part with him for an exorbitant price. Grumbling, the elder Forster paid the man and took the dog back to *Resolution*.

Another two dogs were acquired at the Cape. One officer bought a young terrier bitch while another purchased a large black dog that was a Dutch breed.[10] Being black, the larger dog was likely to have been a crossbreed between the half-wild ridged dogs of the Hottentots that were commonly black or brown, possibly crossed with the common boer or staghound. Rhodesian ridgeback is the name for this crossbreed dog today.

While at the Cape, the Forsters became acquainted with Doctor Anders Sparrman, a young Swedish zoologist who was studying the natural history of the area. Seeing the advantage of having another naturalist on the voyage, especially a young man with a character that Forster perceived as being both dignified and unobtrusive, Forster persuaded Cook to let him hire Sparrman as his assistant. With so little space in the Forsters' cabin, it is difficult to imagine where the water spaniel and Sparrman fitted.

Joseph Shanks, First Lieutenant on *Adventure*, became sick with gout prior to leaving the Cape. Cook promoted Kempe to his First Lieutenant and James Burney transferred to *Adventure* as Second Lieutenant.

AT THE MERCY OF THE WEATHER

They left the Cape on 24 November 1772, the majority of their water casks filled with wine or brandy. The rationale behind this decision was probably that rainwater could be collected but alcohol would be hard to come by. A marine guarded the few casks that contained fresh water. Cook ordered it not to be consumed without his permission. He set an example by washing only in salt water and drinking the water produced by the distilling machine.

The next part of the voyage was routine, the weather cooling the further south they sailed. When not working the men threw lines into the sea or attempted to catch albatrosses with a hook and line, using a greasy piece of sheepskin for bait. The air chilled, the wind blew, and as the seas rose higher the cabins began to leak. A week out of Cape Town squalls of wind and rain battered the rolling ships and the sea forced its way into every cabin. Forster was terrified as waves crashed into the interior of the bucking ship. A large storage box became loose and crashed into the partitions, severely damaging one of the cabins. 'Chairs, glasses, dishes, plates, cup, saucers, bottles etc., were broken.'[11] Forster was concerned about his water spaniel: 'My poor dog wanted to take shelter in my Cabin, against wind, rain, cold and the sea, he found some relief against the three first inconveniences but he could not escape entirely the last.'[12]

Cook ordered Magellan wet jackets and Fearnought trousers be handed to everyone on board *Resolution*. Where most Royal Navy ships of the time carried only a few, there were enough on *Resolution* for everyone on board, from the master to the youngest boy. The ship's milking goats were sheltered in a partition beside the Forsters' cabin. They covered the animal stalls with canvas. Little more could be done to ease the misery of the animals held captive and freezing on the top deck. Three large pigs, two young piglets and two of the Cape's sheep died.

Several more wretched days passed until, finally, the rain stopped and the sun appeared at brief intervals. The men barely had time to put their bedding out to dry when the wind returned, bringing with it more squalls of rain. Empty casks were filled with fresh water. On 6 December, the thermometer fell dramatically and a new storm hit them. The waves roared, hail and rain thundered onto the decks and the ships were thrown around.

Completely at the mercy of the raging ocean, one of the pregnant goats fell and miscarried and most of the remaining livestock from the Cape died. According to Sparrman, the crew asked for the dead animals. Cook refused the request. The Royal Navy's rule was all dead animals were to be thrown overboard. This was to discourage an increase in the mortality of animals when the men desired roast meat. However, not wanting to waste anything on this long unprecedented voyage, and knowing that to throw perfectly good meat overboard was extravagant and irrational, Cook and the officers kept the animals for their own table.[13]

Gradually the sea swell decreased and the sky began to clear. Nevertheless, it grew colder. As the temperature dropped still further each day, three more large pigs died. When the thermometer on deck showed a temperature of 35 degrees Fahrenheit (1.67 degrees Celsius) the breeding ewes, intended as gifts for Māori, became ill. Forster said they 'trembled, panted, and had swollen knees, from cold and the bruises received by the rolling of the ship.' [14]To keep the distressed animals alive, they fed them a gruel mixed with warm water, but they were near death. Fearing the last of the sheep would die, Cook ordered the two ewes and ram housed in the vacant small space beside Johann Forster's cabin. Forster was most indignant, whining 'no more convenient place could be devised than the space between my and the Master's cabin. I was now beset with cattle and stench on both sides, having no other but a thin deal partition full of chinks between me and them.'[15] The straw and hay long gone, the men fed whole and boiled wheat, rice and chickpeas to the sheep and goats. Warm, sheltered from the cold, and with food in their stomachs, their health improved.

Icebergs surrounded the ships, snow began to fall and when it stopped, thick fog obscured their view. Men complained of headaches, swollen glands and fevers. Some took to their beds to escape the monotonous cold, ice and snow. Others drank vast quantities of hot tea, the water smuggled from the replenished casks. A sow delivered nine piglets, but with not even a handful of straw left on board to protect them from the cold, despite the efforts of the men, they died within hours of being born. Sparrman told Cook that when he was in China he had bought pig's milk. Cook saw an opportunity to benefit from the tragedy and promptly ordered the sow be milked. The seamen ignored the order. The bereaved sow had earlier proven to be bad-tempered and aggressive, so no one was willing to do the deed.[16]

Confronted by a solid field of ice and unable to proceed any further south, Cook acknowledged they had gone as far south as they dared. As a source of potential water, he had the men stow twenty tonnes of ice in the longboat. More ice was stored on the quarterdeck and in the empty sheep pen. Finally, Cook gave the order to turn to the north-east.

For two weeks they battled islands of floating ice. Their food supplies consisted only of salt-meat, sauerkraut, a few dead or starving Cape sheep and some equally lean diseased hens and geese. As the ships continued on their north-easterly passage, the weather improved, the air became warmer and the stored ice melted. On the morning of 7 February 1773, the wind increased and carried away *Adventure*'s main topgallant

mast. The following day the temperature increased and the wind stopped. A light drizzle of rain began to fall. When the rain cleared, a dense fog shrouded the ships. *Adventure* and *Resolution* lost sight of each other. So that Furneaux would know where they were, Cook ordered the guns fired every hour. They fired the guns all night, but there was no response from *Adventure*. Earlier, Cook had provided Furneaux with charts, marking places they would rendezvous if they separated. The closest rendezvous was Queen Charlotte Sound. Cook steered *Resolution* towards New Zealand.

RESOLUTION AT DUSKY BAY

When they first sighted the south-west coast of New Zealand, they had been at sea for over seventeen weeks. *Resolution* glided into Dusky Bay (Tamatea, and later named Dusky Sound), a haven of lush woods and stunning evergreens.

Richard Pickersgill went in search of a suitable mooring place and found a deep, narrow passage. They towed *Resolution* into the passage and wedged her between a small island and the mainland. Once *Resolution* was in position, the crew connected her to the shore by a makeshift bridge of fallen logs. By now some of the men and most of the animals were showing symptoms of disease. Men gently carried the ill off the ship and settled them into a camp amongst the bush. Animals were put in makeshift pens on shore. Every day men went out in a small boat to catch fish while others went into the bush to hunt ducks, native pigeons and seals. With access to fresh water, fish, seal's meat and tea brewed from leaves of the mānuka tree, the men quickly recovered their strength.

Dusky Bay in New Zealand, Apr 1773 by William Hodges. The Fletcher Trust Collection, on loan to Auckland Art Gallery Toi o Tāmaki

Most of the animals also began to improve, with one of the ship's cats recuperating more quickly than the others. She made frequent excursions into the woods and soon became fat on the unsuspecting birdlife. Allowed to browse on shore, the goats thrived, but the sheep showed little sign of recovery as their teeth had become loose and there was no grass in the cove, only bush.

The Forsters were keen to try out their water spaniel, but much to their disgust, the timid dog showed little interest in retrieving game. In the first week of April the two Forsters, accompanied by Sparrman, Clerke and Edgcumbe (Lieutenant of Marines), went to Indian Cove (between Indian Island and Long Island) in search of new plants and animal life. They took the officer's black dog with them in the hope they could train him to hunt and eventually to retrieve. At the same time, Cook and some others went off in another direction to hunt for seals. The Forsters' group arrived back in the early evening, minus the black dog. Frightened by the discharge of the first musket that fired, the dog ran off into the woods. They continued their foraging, returning to the same spot later that day in search of him. They could hear him howling, but he would not come to their calls. Cook's group were more successful. They returned about 9 p.m. with three seals, three ducks and a variety of birds.

Some of the men, left at the campsite while the others were out hunting, reported seeing a small quadruped. One said it was yellow and the size of a rabbit. Another described it as a low-legged, long-bodied animal with a pointed snout like a jackal. The evening's discussion focused on the mysterious animal,

with the final consensus being that it was the size of a large cat, resembled a jackal, had short legs, a thick tail and was the colour of a mouse. A cynical Johann Forster, while not saying the men were deliberately lying, inferred they were mistaken. On his frequent excursions into the woods, he had 'never met with anything of this kind.'[17] The younger Forster was less dismissive of the men's story, as another member of the crew had twice reported seeing a brown animal 'something less than a jackal or little fox, about the dawn of morning, sitting on a stump of a tree near our tents, and running off at his approach.'[18] Georg suggested they had seen a wood hen or one of the ship's cats. As Māori were in the vicinity, another possibility is they had seen a Māori dog. For many of the men on board, this was their first landing in New Zealand and they had yet to observe the small breed of Polynesian dog, with its characteristic long body, short legs and a bushy tail that resembled a small fox.

Despite their disbelief of its existence, for several days the men, including Johann Forster, went in search of the mystery animal. During their search, they happened upon a Māori family living in Indian Cove. The family comprised an old man, two elderly women believed to be his wives, three little boys, a boy about fourteen years old and a young woman aged about eighteen to twenty years. On 19 April the Māori family visited the ship. Seeing the sheep and goats in their enclosure, they asked for some. Because there was no grass in Dusky Bay for the sheep to eat, Cook said no. Instead, he invited them on board to see the other animals. The old man and the girl cautiously approached the crude bridge connecting the land to the ship. Following a ceremonial greeting, they stepped on the top deck. When the girl saw the Cape Town geese in their pen she laughed. One of the cats approached her and she leaned over and stroked it. Johann Forster objected, saying she 'stroked the cat the wrong way, though she was shewed it to be the wrong way and against the grain.'[19]

While anchored in Dusky Bay, rain constantly hindered them. When the weather cleared, there would be a flurry of activity. During one break in the weather, a party of officers went with Cook to survey the north-western part of the bay. Crossing paths with the fishing boat that went out each morning, they were surprised and delighted to see the missing black dog in the boat. Hearing him howling, the fishermen had followed the mournful sound and saw him standing on the shore of a nearby point. Still fat and sleek after being absent for two weeks, the dog was quick to leap into the boat and reunite with humans.

The geese that so delighted the girl were Cook's first deliberate introduction of livestock into New Zealand. On 24 April 1773, Cook, Georg Forster, William Anderson (Surgeon's Mate) and some other officers went to an isolated cove with the last of their geese. There they released five geese and a gander while pronouncing over them the Latin phrase: '*Crescite et multiplicamini* ['increase and multiply'].'[20] These were the last of the geese purchased at the Cape. As South Africa has no true indigenous breed of goose,[21] it is likely they were an introduced variety of Chinese goose that was numerous in Cape Town at that time.

They had been in Dusky Bay for over six weeks. Cook decided it was time to leave their lush but very damp haven to rendezvous with *Adventure*. The observatory, forge for ironwork and tents were packed away, and the last of the animals were reloaded on board. Leaving Dusky Bay on 11 May, they proceeded up the west coast of the South Island towards Queen Charlotte Sound.

ADVENTURE ARRIVES

After separating from *Resolution* in the fog, Furneaux sailed to the north until they reached Australia. Anchoring in Tasmania's Adventure Bay, they stayed there for five days to take on board fresh water and wood. While there were signs people resided there, they never saw them. During their exploration of the area, the only wildlife they reported seeing was an opossum[22] and a 'fine white hawk'.[23] Rather than backtrack in the hope they might find *Resolution* in the vast ocean, Furneaux decided to sail for the agreed rendezvous in New Zealand and wait for Cook. First, to see if Tasmania attached to the mainland of Australia, he sailed to the north. Finding the coast treacherous and unwilling to go deep into the Bass Strait, Furneaux mistakenly determined it was a deep bay. Running into some strong, opposing winds, he thought it prudent to make for New Zealand. Assaulted by a storm, their voyage across the Tasman Sea was slow. As soon as they sailed into Queen Charlotte Sound, Furneaux sent a shore party across to Ship Cove to see if *Resolution* had been there. Only finding marks on the trees from Cook's first voyage on *Endeavour*, they set up a camp and Furneaux celebrated their safe arrival by serving an extra half-allowance of brandy. During the night, they could hear the howling of dogs, and people hallooing on the eastern shore, but no Māori approached them. In the morning, the scouts reported finding a deserted 'Hippah' (a pā, Māori fort or village) on the southern end of Motuara Island. Making use of the abandoned shelters, they established a separate settlement for the men who were suffering from scurvy and other illnesses.

For several days, there was no sign of a Māori presence, other than the sounds of the dogs howling from the direction of Arapawa (Arapaoa) Island. This changed on 9 April when the watch on *Adventure* warned a number of canoes were approaching from the south. The largest canoes turned and went into the nearby bay, now known as Resolution Bay, but two other canoes, manned with about eighteen men, approached the ship. Furneaux was surprised to find the Māori familiar with Cook and *Endeavour*, and even more so when they enquired after Tupaia. There appeared to be some confusion in the translation and the Māori became agitated. Furneaux gave up on his inept interpreter (a man who had been on *Endeavour*) and struggling with a translation book written in English and Māori, attempted to explain that Tupaia had died. Finally, understanding Tupaia had died from natural causes and not been killed by the Europeans, the men left, paddling towards Resolution Bay. They returned the next day to trade, accompanied by fifty more people. Three days later they were joined by a further 120 Māori. Their leader was the paramount chief, Te Ringapuhi.[24]

With winter approaching, Furneaux prepared to spend the next few months in Queen Charlotte Sound. He ordered *Adventure* be moored closer to the beach, stores transferred to the land and the spars

and lumber of the decks be caulked. He had *Adventure* covered in a sheathing to preserve her hull and rigging. With his ship now retired for the winter, Furneaux introduced European horticultural skills to local Māori and together they created vegetable gardens.

At sunrise on 18 May, the sound of guns firing rudely awoke them. It was Cook's signal: *Resolution* had arrived.

THE RENDEZVOUS

Cook's immediate concern was the health of Furneaux's ailing men living in the derelict huts on Motuara Island. The huts were crawling with fleas, lice and other vermin, including rats, which were now prolific on the island. He ordered an antiscorbutic diet for those still showing symptoms of scurvy and ordered Furneaux to get his men to remove the vermin. They put large jars in the ground, level with the surface, into which the rats would fall during the night. Georg Forster said that great numbers would run backwards and forwards across the jars 'and great numbers of them were caught in this manner.'[25] Sparrman was disgusted when a man wanted to cook and eat the rats. A medical doctor, he warned that during autopsies he had discovered lice in the stomachs of corpses, 'clinging together in large clusters or nests; also between the membranes, inside the many blisters into which they have eaten their way'.[26]

Cook ordered *Resolution*'s livestock be moved to the shore and penned next to the *Adventure*'s main tent. Cook had no intention of wasting time, spending winter in New Zealand. He ordered Furneaux to have *Adventure* and her crew prepared for sea as quickly as possible.

H.M.S. Resolution arrives at Ship Cove, Queen Charlotte Sound, 17 May, 1773. Geoffrey C. Ingleton 1953. Pictures Collection nla.gov.au/nla.cat-vn595816. Permission from Michaela King.

The following days were spent collecting scurvy grass and celery for the animals. On 23 May 1773 they found the ewe and ram dead. This was a great loss as they were the last of their breeding sheep. While the deaths were attributed to them eating a poisonous plant, it is possible the sheep never fully recovered from the hazardous voyage. Alternatively, perhaps some extremely hungry men, starved of fresh meat for months, played a part in their deaths. Whatever the cause, no doubt the men dined on mutton that evening. They shared their meal with five Māori, previously unknown to Cook. Anderson identified their dinner guests as the chief, Towahanga (Te Wahanga)[27], and his companions as Kotughaia, Koghoaa (Koogooaa)[28], Khoaa and Kollakh (of Ngāi Tahu).[29] Most of the diary entries for 23 May 1773 mention this group of Māori leaving in the evening loaded with presents. Rather than the usual offering of iron nails and trinkets, however, Villiers says the captains offered their visitors a gift of breeding hogs and a pair of breeding goats.[30] We now know that Koghoaa resided at Grass Cove (Wharehunga Bay) on Arapawa Island.[31] The group returned several days later, minus the animals, bringing others with them including a boy estimated to be about twelve years old by the name of Taupuaperua (Taiwahirooa)[32]. Unlike the others, who would only drink water sweetened with sugar, Taupuaperua drunk the Madeira wine and became intoxicated.

On 1 June another group of Māori approached them, all strangers to Cook and his men. They brought with them a number of dogs to trade. Māori kept the dogs in the canoe with a string tied around their middle. Forster described the dogs as being a rough,

longhaired sort, with pricked ears. They came in a variety of colours, 'some were spotted, some black, and others perfectly white.'[33] This description differs slightly from Banks and Parkinson's earlier description of a small, ugly, fox-like creature with a short bushy tail. Once they had traded their dogs for nails and other European goods, the strangers paddled towards the south.

Believing there were no Māori around to observe what they were doing, Furneaux, his Second Lieutenant, James Burney, and some of *Adventure*'s crew rowed across to Cannibal Cove where they released two breeding sows and a large black boar into the woods. One of the sows was already heavily pregnant. Burney later wrote 'if the Zealanders do not find them out and destroy them there may be a fine breed in a short time.'[34] The following day Cook, Furneaux and the Forsters secreted a breeding pair of goats into Arapawa Island's East Bay, where they released them into the woods. A cynic might say Cook's purpose of releasing livestock into the wild of Queen Charlotte Sound was for the benefit of future explorers. A note recorded in Cook's journal suggests he put the animals there to benefit Māori, who he knew were cannibals. Cook may have connected the act of cannibalism to a scarcity of meat. 'The pigs and goats which might come from those we left here must be considered as a future benefit for the country and they run a good chance enough to thrive well, for there is plenty of food here for both kinds of animals.'[35] As most of the South African animals perished in the Southern Ocean, it is probable the goats were an unimproved Old English breed, predominant in England during Cook's voyages.

Māori Boy and a Goat

On 4 June 1773 they celebrated King George III's thirty-fifth birthday. Invited to the celebration were some Māori, including Towahanga, his son Khoaa and daughter Koparnee.[36] Arriving at the festivity, Towahanga presented Cook with some gifts for the king. These included some green nephrite stones shaped into chisels and blades of hatchets. In return for the gifts, Towahanga indicated he would like Khoaa to have one of Cook's fancy white shirts. Cook initially thought Towahanga was giving him Khoaa as a gift, but realising his mistake, gave the boy a dress shirt. The naked Khoaa promptly put it on. Anderson, who was present at the time, wrote: 'The boy was so highly delighted with the new garment that he went all over the ship, presenting himself before everyone who came in his way.'[37] Khoaa, so focused on showing off in the shirt, did not see Old Will, the ram goat. Old Will took offence at the absurd figure of Khoaa lost in the ample turns and folds of Cook's shirt. The sturdy mountain goat stepped in the boy's way and raised himself up on his hind legs. He butted his head full against the startled Khoaa, sending the boy sprawling on the deck. Georg Forster, who was watching, said, 'The unsuccessful efforts which the boy made to rise, together with his loud lamentations, so provoked the goat, that he prepared to repeat the compliment, and would probably have silenced this knight of the rueful countenance if some of our people had not intervened.'[38]

Khoaa's face and hands now covered with dirt, the shirt filthy, Georg picked up the crying boy and took him to his father. Rather than comforting his son, Georg said Khoaa's actions provoked his father's indignation and he 'received several blows as a punishment of his folly, before we could make his peace.'[39] At Cook's instructions, some of the officers cleaned the shirt and washed the humiliated boy, which the senior Forster suggested 'perhaps had never happened to him before during his life, and thus succeeded to restore him to his former tranquillity.'[40] Towahanga took off his own cloak and carefully rolled the dirty shirt inside its folds. He left the ship with Khoaa and Koparnee trailing behind. The celebrations continued into the evening when the marines, lined up on shore, fired their guns in honour of the king's birthday. The celebration concluded with bonfires and fireworks.

Ludicrous circumstance on board Resolution, by W. F. Mavor

New Zealand to Tahiti

Cook informed Furneaux that they would sail to the east in search of the new land, as far south as latitude 41 degrees. They would go to Tahiti to gather more supplies and return to New Zealand before again plunging south as far as they could go. On 7 June, *Resolution* and *Adventure* sailed out of Queen Charlotte Sound into Cook Strait. On *Resolution* were the three dogs purchased at the Cape of Good Hope: the Forsters' water spaniel, the terrier, now in pup to the spaniel,[41] and the large black dog that had absconded and returned when they were in Dusky Bay. Also on board were some Māori dogs and the ships' cats, now fat from the abundance of unwary native birds. Added to this menagerie were a small herd of goats, some large pigs and at least three of the castrated Cape sheep that had survived the voyage from Cape Town to Queen Charlotte Sound. Useless for breeding, the wethers were a food source, which is probably why Cook wrote of the last ewe and ram dying in Ship Cove. Renewing his search for the non-existent, great Southern Continent, Cook gave the order to proceed to the east, then turn southwards to explore parts of the sea that were unknown to him.

Within a week of leaving any port, most of any remaining fresh provisions were inedible. Rather than eat the salted meat, the officers on *Resolution* decided to slaughter and roast one of the dogs. They selected the now fat, black dog that had caused them so much trouble in Dusky Bay. Sparrman justified this choice, writing: 'We resolved upon killing a fat, though ugly Dutch dog, before the scurvy, together with the short commons of the ship, should render his flesh unfit for eating. Already used in our run between the Cape and New Zealand to put up with sheep that had died of the scurvy or other disorders, diseased hens and geese, we certainly were not now in a condition to turn up our noses at a roasted dog, which was really nice and well-tasted.[42] Roasted with garlic, the dog's legs were served to Captain Cook and the junior officers. The senior officers and gentlemen dined on the rib and shoulders, and the leftovers baked into a pie for the next day.[43] The men were astounded to find only a very young New Zealand puppy would eat the fleshy bones when they were offered to the dogs. Johann Forster said the puppy 'had certainly had no opportunity of tasting anything but the mother's milk before we purchased it, however it eagerly devoured a portion of the flesh and bones of the dog on which we dined today, while several others of the European breed taken on board at the Cape, turned from it without touching it.[44] Unwilling to slaughter another dog for the crew, they opened their store of 'Experimental beef'. The butcher had made experimental beef from the bullock they slaughtered after leaving St Jago ten months earlier. He had skinned the bullock, cut its meat into small pieces, and preserved it in salt and sugar. Unfortunately, as the beef aged it became rancid. Johann Forster grumbled, 'it grew worse than the common salt beef, and became as it were, nauseous.[45] Nevertheless, they ate it before opening the barrels of salted beef loaded in England.

On *Resolution*, the routine of daily baths, scrubbing decks and serving antiscorbutic foods continued, but it seems Furneaux did not follow Cook's strict example. Three weeks after they left New Zealand, an officer informed Cook there was sickness on board *Adventure*. Twenty of her men had scurvy, the cook had died of it, and Furneaux was unwell.

They were now in winter and the weather was challenging for both men and animals. Mountainous waves hurled the ships around. On 9 July a young goat attempted to reach the hay stored in the longboat by climbing onto one of the booms (a pole that runs horizontally along the foot of a sail). The ship suddenly lurched and the goat fell overboard. The officers and crew went to great lengths to save the young ram buck, born on *Resolution* before they had reached the Cape of Good Hope. Johann Forster watched the animal's struggle from the top deck: 'He swam at first hard, we brought to and hoisted a boat out, but he was drowned before they could take him up. We tried to chafe him in the Galley by rubbing and fire, and I advised to have a tobacco-smoke glyster applied [a syringe into the bowels], but all proved ineffectual.'[46] Starved of fresh provisions, there is little doubt the officers and gentlemen received fresh goat meat that night.

By the end of July 1773, the number of sick on board *Adventure* had increased to twenty-eight, more than a third of the ship's company. Cook was furious that Furneaux had allowed his men to get in such a state. He sent an aged seaman who had lost two of his fingers, William Chapman, to *Adventure* as their replacement cook. Cook instructed Chapman to feed the sick sauerkraut. Climbing down to where the sick lay, he found the miserable wretches, suspended in rows, with not more than fourteen inches of space between them. They had little light. The portholes closed, deprived of fresh air,

the men inhaled gases coming from their own filth and diseased bodies. Vermin crawled over the men and bred in the piles of faeces that surrounded them. On receiving this report, faced with the probability of more deaths, and with one of his own men showing symptoms, Cook decided to steer for Tahiti.

THE CANNIBAL PUPPY

Other than fish and seabirds, the next fresh meat eaten on *Resolution* was 4 August. The terrier bitch from the Cape delivered ten puppies, one of which was stillborn. To the elder Forster's horror, the New Zealand dog that had earlier devoured the remains of the roasted black dog fell upon the dead puppy 'and ate of it with a ravenous appetite.' Disgusted, Forster interpreted the starving animal's actions as 'proof how far education may go in producing and propagating new instincts in animals.' Forster went on to express his prejudice and ignorance, claiming European dogs never fed on the meat of their own species, as they abhorred it. Incredibly, he rationalised that Māori dogs, 'in all likelihood, are trained up from their earliest age to eat the remains of their master's meals; they are therefore used to feed upon fish, their own species, and perhaps human flesh; and what was only owing to habit at first, may have become instinct by length of time.'[47] Forster must have taken a breath long enough to realise the puppy had come on the ship straight off its mother. He continued: 'This was remarkable in our cannibal-dog, for he came on board so young, that he could not have been weaned long enough to acquire a habit of devouring his own species, and much less of eating human flesh.' In support of his ludicrous theory that Māori dogs were born cannibals, Forster recalled an earlier event: 'one of our seamen having cut his finger, held it out to the dog, who fell to greedily, licked it, and then began to bite into it.'[48]

As they sailed to the north the weather improved, the temperature rose and tropical birds began to appear. The ships stopped at several small islands where they obtained fresh fruit and the occasional pig. With fresh air and fresh food, the sick men began to recover. Cook was unable to acquire more than the occasional pig. At last, Tahiti was within their sights. Wary of the coral reefs and atolls surrounding Tahiti, Cook cautiously directed the two sloops to Vaitepiha Bay (Oaitepeha) on the northern tip of the island.

AROUND THE PACIFIC ISLANDS

With many of the men still sick and exhausted, Cook's immediate priority was the acquisition of fresh water, vegetables and meat. The Tahitians refused to provide them with live animals, although they willingly offered them water, vegetables and fruit in abundance. The chief, Aree, told his people to take the live animals into the country and away from the ships.[49] Cook asked why they could not buy livestock. Aree explained that over the past five to six years, the large numbers of hogs and fowls carried off the island by European ships had decimated their numbers. The visiting ships included *Dolphin*, commanded by Wallis, the Frenchman, Monsieur Bougainville's two ships, *Endeavour* (there for months), and wrote Cook, 'other French ships since then, have at a moderate computation, consumed 2000 Hogs besides fowls.' Unknown to

Cook and Furneaux, nine months earlier the Spaniard, Don Domingo Boenechea, captain of the Spanish ship *Aguila*, introduced a pair of nanny goats and a kid, as well as a cock, a hen, two pairs of pigeons and some guinea pigs on Tahiti's southern coast.[50]

Cook managed to purchase a few animals two days before the ships sailed, sufficient to provide the ships' companies with three fresh meals.

When they arrived at their old anchorage in Matavai Bay, they were able to purchase nine more pigs. On 27 August, Otoo (or Otou), a Tahitian chief, climbed on board *Resolution* with a live hog to trade. Offered a male and two female goats for the hog, Otoo happily accepted. Then Otoo saw the Forsters' spaniel and asked for that too. At the captains' insistence, Johann reluctantly handed the dog over to him. The chief ordered one of his servants to carry the dog 'filthy with tar and grease [to the village] and thus he got the important position of dog-bearer to his Otahaitean Majesty.'[51] Later, Cook and Furneaux presented the chief with the last three, rather emaciated wethered sheep from the Cape, and some cats. The chief gave them a large hog each in return. Tired of hearing Forster complain that he received nothing in return for the spaniel, Cook asked if the Forsters could receive a hog for their dog. The chief sent for another hog, but only a very small pig came back. Otoo told Cook to give the small pig to the Forsters. Johann was not impressed. He complained it was too little and sickly, and refused it. Otoo ordered the little pig taken away. The servant returned with a hog, larger than the ones given to Cook and Furneaux, and handed it to the Forsters.

A Human Sacrifice, in a Morai, in Otaheite: – in the presence of Captain Cook. By Webber. In Anderson 1784: 487

The Forsters' spaniel would survive to breed with the Tahitian Poe dogs. Maximo Rodriguez, a marine on the *Aguila*, recorded in his journal that when the Spanish arrived at Matavai Bay early in July 1775, he was shown animals left by Cook, including spaniels, goats, pigs, a goose and two sheep.

Cook heard there was to be a religious ceremony that involved human sacrifice. He asked Otoo if he and some of men could attend. Otoo agreed and escorted Cook, Anderson and Webber, along with a half-starved dog, some men and a few boys, to a small island. Four priests said prayers over a male corpse, which began the ritual of sacrifice. They killed the dog by twisting its neck; its hair was burnt off and the entrails thrown into the fire. The dog's blood was smeared over the corpse and the corpse then placed in front of the priest. The remains of the dog went on a scaffold next to the decomposing carcasses of two dogs and three pigs.

The ceremony over, they buried the body of the sacrificial victim in front of the marae.[52] Soon after returning to the village, Cook informed Otoo they were leaving. Having received fresh meat, greens and water, the sick were recovering, but Cook knew they would need more fresh meat if they were to remain healthy for the voyage back to New Zealand.

HUAHINE

On 1 September 1773 they sailed for Huahine, taking with them Porio, an intelligent young Tahitian who Cook thought would make a useful interpreter. Two days later they anchored in Fare Harbour on the west side of Huahine, where they purchased fifty hogs. This was still not enough to sustain them all. Knowing there were more hogs on the island, the captains sent the men out in the boats, armed with beads and nails, around the island to buy more. By the evening they had acquired 200 hogs, and by the end of the next day, this number had swelled to almost 500. While scouting for livestock, Georg Forster became intrigued by the way the islanders treated their dogs, which were in abundance: 'The women here commonly carry [the dogs] in their arms as if they had little children: and these animals are so much used to it, that they lie on their backs, and sleep as quietly as possible.'[53] They acquired at least twelve Huahine dogs, which Georg Forster said were short and varying in size from a small lap dog to the largest spaniel. He described them as having a broad head, 'the snout pointed, the eyes very small, the ears upright, and their hair rather long, lank, hard, and of different colours, but most commonly white and brown. They seldom if ever barked, but howled sometimes, and were shy of strangers to a degree of aversion.'[54] His father said the dogs, as well as ten cocks they bought, were 'sea provisions' and the hogs were for immediate consumption.

Every available space taken up with grunting, cackling or howling animals, Forster became anxious about where they would all fit. Ignoring his concerns, the men went looking for even more livestock. For the next few days the mariners toured the island, walking to villages and buying up pigs. Deviating from their established tracks to villages, Sparrman and Georg Forster walked overland and came across a large number of hogs, dogs and fowl, all wandering about at their leisure. They were intrigued to see an elderly woman handfeeding a pig with some sour fermented breadfruit paste. Georg

Dog in a canoe in 'A view of Huaheine' by John Webber. from Anderson's A New, authentic, and complete collection of voyages round the world …., published for Alex. Hogg, London 1784. (Accessed Alexander Turnbull library)

described how she did it: 'she held the pig with one hand, and offered it a tough pork's skin, but as soon as it opened the mouth to snap at it, she contrived to throw a handful of the sour paste in, which the little animal would not take without this stratagem.'[55] They also came across a middle-aged woman, having recently lost her own baby and her breasts rich with milk, breastfeeding a dog. 'We were witnesses of a remarkable instance of kindness when we saw a middle-aged woman, whose breasts were full of milk, offering them to a little puppy which had been trained up to suck them. We were so much surprised at this sight, that we could not help expressing our dislike of it; but she smiled at our observation, and added, that she suffered little pigs to do the same service.'

Satisfied they had sufficient provisions for the next few months, the ships jammed with livestock, they left Huahine behind on 7 September and steered for Ra'iātea. On *Adventure* was Mae, who they called Omai, a man who hung around the ship from the moment she anchored. 'He expressed the greatest desire to go to Britainia'[56] wrote Furneaux. Omai was a native of Ra'iātea. When a group from Bora Bora (a small island north-west of Tahiti) had invaded his island the previous year, Omai fled to Huahine.

RA'IĀTEA

Their passage took one day. Between both ships, as well as pigs they carried thirty dogs and more than fifty cocks. However, they were short of vegetables and other greens. A heavily tattooed Bora Bora chief welcomed them. While Omai stayed on *Adventure* with some of the crew, the rest of the men went ashore. Searching for plants, Forster was surprised to

come across a cemetery for the locals' dogs, an indication that dogs were valued pets. They were at Ra'iātea for over a week, long enough for Omai to be attacked by some Bora Bora warriors, and for Porio to fall in love with a local girl. Before they left, another Polynesian interpreter, Hitihiti, replaced Porio. The men called him Odiddy. He would be Cook's interpreter and Omai would continue sailing with Furneaux on *Adventure*.

Their thirst for livestock was insatiable. While they were at Ra'iātea, the trade for pigs continued. One day some islanders stole a bag belonging to John (Jack) Rowe, Master's Mate on *Adventure*. Some of his mates seized a hog to compensate for the theft. The owners of the pig did not want to give it up and chased the sailors, who were holding tightly to the squealing animal, towards their ship. As they ran along the beach, they saw some pigs loose on the hills. They stopped and collected these too.

The men enjoyed their stay at Ra'iātea. They socialised with the women and admired the Bora Bora warriors' strength and tattoos. Some of *Resolution*'s junior officers decided to emulate them. They had a large star tattooed on their chest and called themselves 'The Knights of Tahiti'.[57] Part of the initiation ritual to be a member entailed eating a select part of a roasted dog.

By the time they left Ra'iātea, the decks were swarming with dogs, junglefowl and hundreds of pigs. There were pigs in stalls and pens; there were even pigs crammed in crates in the cargo hold. What they did not have, however, was sufficient food to sustain all the animals on the long voyage ahead. They sailed around some nearby islands looking for greens. The islanders offered them hogs, but there was no pig food. They bought the hogs anyhow and continued their search. Cook sent Pickersgill out to find a source of food for the pigs. On 14 September Pickersgill got lucky. The nearby island of Taha'a (Otaha) had an abundance of fruit, yams, bananas and other fresh greens suitable for the livestock, which they purchased.

Leaving the Society Islands fully provisioned, they carried with them close to 300 pigs in each ship, as well as a large number of poultry and dogs. With so many bananas stored on the poop deck (the roof of a cabin at the stern) it looked like a miniature orchard. This bounty was not to last. The pigs were crammed so close together in the pens that they began to suffocate. To allow more room for the healthier animals, Cook ordered the weakest hogs slaughtered. The meat had to be salted and stored before it became too rotten. The vegetables and bananas became inedible and the roosters and hens, unused to eating the ships' dried biscuits, became ill and began to die. The pampered dogs they purchased at Huahine became depressed. They refused to eat or drink, and died. This was a time of feast for the men on *Resolution* and *Adventure*.

TONGA (COOK'S FRIENDLY ISLANDS)

On 2 October they approached Nomuka, one of the Tongan islands and named Rotterdam by Tasman, where they were able to purchase more bananas and yams, as well as some coconuts. They also acquired another seventy hogs on this island and quite a few large cocks. So impressed were they with this island and the animals, that the artist, William Hodges, sketched it.

In the foreground, Hodges has illustrated the small Polynesian pig with its long snout, straight tail and small pointed ears.

POLYNESIAN PIGS

In his study of Oceania's feral pigs for his Doctorate in Zoology, Diong refers to William Hodges' sketch 'A view in the Island of Rotterdam' as the closest illustration of the ancestral, indigenous Polynesian pig.[58] He also claims the Polynesian pig most probably derived from the East Asiatic boar, *Sus scrofa vittatus*, commonly known as the banded pig. He based this hypothesis on the pigs' predominant physical characteristics: a relatively small size, long snout, short erect ears, primarily black coat with bristled hairs and woolly undercoat, an arched back, high tail, deer-like feet, long legs, and juvenile striping present in the young.

However, these were not the only pig breed in the South Pacific seen during Cook's second voyage. Prior to European arrival, crossbreeding of pigs was already occurring in the Pacific Islands. Forster observed the small but fatter Chinese pigs in Tahiti: 'The hogs of that breed which we call the Chinese, having a short body, short legs, belly hanging down almost to the ground, the ears erect, and very few thin hairs on the body; their meat is the most juicy, and their fat the most agreeable and the least cloying I ever tasted.'[59]

Hodges, William, 744-1797. *A view in the Island of Rotterdam. Alexander Turnbull Library, Wellington, New Zealand. Ref. A-111-088*

Forster described the Chinese pigs as being numerous in the Society Islands – almost every house had them. He also saw an abundance of the Chinese hogs at the Marquesas and Tasman's Amsterdam (Tongatapu) islands, but spotted only a few on the western islands of the New Hebrides (Vanuatu). One study suggests the Chinese breed came from the Canton District of China and Indo-China into the Pacific Islands just prior to Cook's voyages.[60] This conclusion is supported by other findings which, using DNA analysis, claim Chinese indigenous pig breeds have a single origin: South East China.[61]

Dogs and Bats in Tonga

While the Tongan islands had a large number of Polynesian and Chinese pigs, they had no dogs. Cook invited an elderly man to dinner on board *Resolution*. After they had dined, Cook, Furneaux and the Forsters prepared to return him to the shore. As he stepped out of the cabin, the man saw a Tahitian dog running about the deck. He became so excited he started clapping his hands against his chest saying the word 'goorree' repeatedly. They were so surprised that he knew the name of an animal that existed in New Zealand (kurī; which the Englishmen pronounced 'goure') and not Tonga; they gave him a breeding pair.[62]

Resolution and *Adventure* were again brimming with livestock and fresh food. The men built a temporary stage on the quarterdeck to accommodate the extra produce. With summer approaching, Cook decided it was time to return to New Zealand where they would take on wood and fresh water, then proceed to the south in search of the Southern Continent. As *Resolution* and *Adventure* coasted out to the open sea, they left behind the canoes that had surrounded the ships. The men on *Resolution* were too busy to notice. The temporary stage on the quarterdeck collapsed under the weight of bananas and coconuts. To stop the unpenned animals from gorging themselves, they needed every spare hand.

On 4 October they stopped at the northern point of Tongatapu and explored the area. Sparrman was horrified to encounter a plague of bats that were the size of a man's shoe. He claimed they not only ate huge amounts of the islanders' fruit but also drank human blood. (He later identified the bats as the species *Vespertilio vampyrus*, an animal that feeds exclusively on fruit, flowers and nectar.)[63] There were thousands of the bats hanging from the tall casuarina (similar to the Australian pine) trees. Some hung by the hooks on their wings and others by their feet. To the delight of the watching Tongans, Sparrman and the Forsters shot at the branches of one tree, killing a large number of the bats.

Discovered in *Resolution*'s pump-well a week after leaving Tonga was one of the Huahine dogs. He had been there without any food for nearly forty days. He was paralysed and passing blood from the anus.[64] Cook ordered the animal put out of its misery and its body thrown overboard. The pitifully emaciated dog was not worth eating. Deeply affected by the agony the dog must have experienced, the men agreed they would only purchase young dogs in the future. Puppies were less likely to pine and refuse to eat.[65]

By 16 October 1773 they had run out of fresh food. Cook put the crew on reduced rations to conserve what food they had. With no more fruit, vegetables or hay for the animals, they fed dried peas to the sheep and goats. With the pigs' staple diet being the men's leftovers, there was not enough food for all the pigs. The pigs began to starve. As they became too weak to walk on the deck without falling over, the butcher slaughtered them and preserved the meat.

Back to New Zealand

Cook's plan on reaching New Zealand was to make for Tolaga Bay. He knew there was water there and he wanted to leave animals and vegetable seeds for Māori. However, the weather turned against them, forcing Cook to alter their course. With the slower *Adventure* lagging behind, the crew on *Resolution* were the first to observe New Zealand on the horizon. Early in the morning of 21 October 1773, *Resolution* neared Portland Island (Waikawa) on Māhia Peninsula. They could see people watching them from the beach, but no canoes came out to meet them. Cook decided to push towards the south. *Adventure* caught up with *Resolution* and they sailed together towards Cape Kidnappers. The following morning, three canoes put off from the nearby shore and approached *Resolution* as she passed Bare Island (Te Motu-o-Kura).

The Māori in the first canoe brought fish, which they exchanged for cloth and nails. The second canoe, more ornately carved than the first, contained two chiefs. The principal

of these two chiefs was Tuanui.[66] Cook invited the chiefs on board, signalling for Furneaux to continue on to Queen Charlotte Sound. Cook then escorted his guests to the Great Cabin, and gave them seeds, nails and animals. Tuanui appeared interested only in the nails and having Hodges draw his portrait. Cook was eager to catch up with Furneaux and escorted his visitors to where their canoe was waiting. Next to the railing were two Pacific Island boars and two sows, as well as six junglefowl: four hens and two cocks. Watching the animals loaded into his canoe, Tuanui promised Cook they would be cared for and allowed to breed.[67]

When the Māori were gone they sailed after *Adventure*. The wind began to change. Within a few hours a gale hammered them. *Resolution* lost one of her masts. *Adventure* was also battling the winds and huge swells. For two days the ships struggled against the force of the hurricane. They briefly came together off Cape Palliser (Kawakawa). Both at the mercy of the north-westerly winds, they were again separated, this time with *Resolution* ahead of *Adventure*. Powerless in the face of the storm, for days the ships heaved, rolled and shuddered. Catching glimpses of the land but unable to get round Cape Turnagain, *Adventure*'s men renamed it 'Cape Turn and be damnd'.[68] Such was the ferociousness of the storm that Omai huddled in fear and Furneaux was unable to hide his own terror. As the storm raised the sea, waves broke over *Resolution*, time after time crashing against the pens that contained the pitiful livestock. During the fury of the storm, a heavy chest lashed to the upper deck dislodged, crashing to the deck and narrowly missing fourteen-year-old

Alexander Hood. As the sea rushed through the hatches and doors, men lurched through six to eight inches of water. Breaking waves crashed against the windows of the Great Cabin. Cook ordered the windows replaced with dead-lights (shutters). This action disturbed a scorpion hiding in a crack by the window. As *Resolution* convulsed and heaved, someone had to get rid of the agitated, venomous animal. On 29 October *Resolution* and *Adventure* came within sight of each other for the last time on this voyage.

The wind made a sudden shift. Cook ordered *Resolution* be kept close to shore while Furneaux sought safety out to sea. The tempest raged for two more days, and then the sea quietened. Cook steered *Resolution* towards Queen Charlotte Sound. Nearing Cape Campbell (Te Karaka) on the South Island, the fickle winds changed, pushing her to the north-west. *Resolution*'s sails and rigging in shreds from the earlier storm, Cook directed her into an inlet on the east side of Cape Teerawhitte (Terawhiti). There they would shelter from the wind and keep an eye out for *Adventure*. They dropped anchor near Pillar Rock, to the south-west of Barrett Reef (Tangihanga-a-Kupe) at the entrance to Wellington Harbour (Te Whanganui-a-Tara).

As they waited, some canoes approached them from both sides of the harbour. According to Irishman and Gunner's Mate, John Marra, some of these men were those that had approached *Resolution* on 22 October. Five Māori climbed on board, bringing dried fish with them. Cook gave them some yams, demonstrating how to plant them, another sow and boar and some cocks and hens.[69] The group now had three

boars, three sows, four cocks and six hens, sufficient breeding stock to start a small farm.

The wind changed to the south at three in the afternoon. They made for the safety of Cook Strait as Cook was unwilling to risk being trapped in the harbour.

SILENCE IN SHIP COVE

There was no sign of *Adventure* or her men at Ship Cove. While the men were busy carrying stores from the ship to the campsite, some officers, the naturalists and some marines went across to Motuara Island to check the gardens they had planted previously. They found the radishes and turnips had gone to seed, the potatoes pulled up by Māori, and the peas and beans eaten by rats. However, there were plenty of carrots and cabbages to take back to the camp. When they returned to Ship Cove a group of Māori who Cook recognised from the *Endeavour* voyage greeted them. Among them was the old man, Goubiah. Cook was delighted to meet up with his old friends and asked them if they knew what had become of the animals. They told him the goats, hogs and poultry had been eaten. While Cook was lamenting the failure of his plan to stock New Zealand with livestock, they lost their last buck. Forster described the buck as the 'the old He-Goat'[70] so it was probably Old Will.

Old Will and a doe were browsing near the tents when the buck suddenly began to convulse. He recovered and the men put the spasms down to him having eaten some stinging nettles. Believing he would leave the nettles alone in the future, they left them to browse in the same area. The buck had more convulsions two days later. In a fit bordering

HMS Resolution, Captain Jas Cook, and HMS Adventure, Captain Furneaux, off Cape Palliser, New Zealand, in

1773. Matthew Clayton, 1898, oil on canvas. Auckland Art Gallery Toi o Tāmaki, gift of William Aitken, 1899

*Cook Strait, New Zealand, circa 1884, London, by Nicholas Chevalier. Purchased 2003. Te Papa (2003-0034-1).
Looking towards the entrance of Wellington Harbour,*

with Matiu/Somes Island in the foreground, Mākaro/Ward Island and Pencarrow to the left. Barrett Reef is clearly visible in the centre of the painting.

on madness, Old Will ran off along the beach, the doe close at his heels. The doe returned later that day, but they never saw the buck again. The men searched for him in the nearby woods but found no trace of him. They presumed the distressed animal had eaten a poisonous plant, run into the sea and drowned. This was a reasonable assumption, as given his symptoms of two seizures, it is possible the buck had eaten the plant tutu, the toot plant of New Zealand (*Coriaria arborea*). However, given the time between the two episodes and the description of him running away rather than convulsing where he lay, it is equally likely the nettle or native bees had stung him. At the time of this incident, there were upwards of 150 canoes in the Sound. Rather than the goat drowning, it is more likely Māori rescued and kept him.

There was no time to grieve the loss of the buck. Summer was approaching and they needed to prepare for the voyage to the subantarctic waters, which they knew would be arduous. Some of the men cut down some trees for wood. Others opened and checked casks containing dried food. Cook was horrified to hear the casks containing bread and biscuits had water seepage. While attributed to the poor quality of the timber, it is reasonable to assume rats had nibbled them. When they opened the casks, the majority of bread (nearly 2000 kilograms)[71] was so damaged it was inedible. With nothing wasted, what was soft and considered potentially edible by humans was rebaked 'and that which was utterly unfit for the men's use, was preserved to feed the hogs and fowls.'[72]

During these preparations, some strangers settled near the tents. Early the next morning

the group was gone, along with a heavy coat and a bag of seamen's clothes. Cook was furious. Accompanied by Māori and some of his men, they found the thieves, along with the stolen clothes, in a nearby cove. Cook went from anger to ecstasy. Amongst the Māori was the younger of the two sows left in Cannibal Cove by Furneaux. It was lame in one hind leg, otherwise healthy and very tame. Cook realised that if she was alive, the other livestock had likely survived too. Cook asked the chief, Tiratou, about the other animals. He indicated the older sow was somewhere towards the east and the boar remained somewhere near Cannibal Cove, and that Goubiah had eaten all the goats and poultry.[73] Upset at his old friend's treachery, but delighted with the condition of the young sow, Cook gave Tiratou a Polynesian sow and a boar, and two jungle cocks and hens. Several canoes carrying more people they had not met before came into the cove. The strangers settled into a small bay near the tents. In the morning the strangers and six of the small water casks were gone. Cook went to Tiratou's cove to find he and his people were gone. They had left behind some of their dogs as well as the Polynesian boar Cook had given to them. While annoyed at the loss of the water casks, Cook was delighted to have the pig back as there were no more live boars on *Resolution*.

On 10 November an extravagantly carved canoe slipped alongside *Resolution*. Towahanga, with his wife, son Khoaa, and daughter Kopare (this was probably Koparnee who was on *Resolution* earlier) had come to trade.[74]

As the days passed, Cook became increasingly concerned about the fate of

Adventure. He climbed the hill on Arapawa Island's East Bay but could not see much due to a thick haze. Cook decided to go in search of his support ship. First, he was determined to introduce livestock into the wild. The deteriorating weather provided him with an opportunity, as Māori left them to seek shelter elsewhere. On the morning of 22 November, seeing only one small canoe in the northern part of the Sound, Cook, Sparrman and the two Forsters went deep into West Bay (Endeavour Inlet) and carried to the shore three sows, the last boar, two cocks and two hens. They trekked into the woods and found an isolated marshy spot where they released the animals, along with sufficient food to last them about twelve days.[75] Returning to Ship Cove, they released more cocks and hens into the woods. A war party appeared, claiming success in a hunting trip in Admiralty Bay (to the west of Queen Charlotte Sound). They had with them some meat, which they laughingly claimed to be from a buck.[76] Some of the crew went on shore and found the remains of the cannibal feast – the victim was a young boy. The head and bones of the boy were on the ground and his heart was stuck on a forked stick attached to the ornate canoe. While the sight traumatised most of the men, Lieutenant Pickersgill purchased the head for a couple of nails and took it back to *Resolution*. Clerke took the head and sliced off some of the meat, which he cooked and offered to some Māori. Some crew vomited as the Māori ate it. Cook, Wales, the Forsters and Odiddy arrived at this moment. Odiddy was horrified and revolted, not only at the act of cannibalism, but also at the Europeans cooking and offering the meat.

Cook decided it was time to leave. He wrote a note in case Furneaux should arrive after they left. In the note, he gave the route he intended to follow, and then put the note in a bottle, which was sealed and buried under the root of a tree. They attached a wooden sign to the tree: 'Look Underneath'.

They sailed out of the Sound on 25 November 1773. Near Cape Terrawittee, they moved close inshore and fired the guns in the hope Furneaux might respond. Continuing towards the east along the coast, every hour they fired the guns, stopping only when it became dark. The following morning they resumed their search, doubled Cape Palliser then steered for Cape Campbell (Te Karaka). Discovering no sign of *Adventure* and receiving no response from all their signals, Cook gave the order to change their course to the south-southeast. As Cook renewed his search for the Great Southern Continent, *Adventure* was sailing towards Queen Charlotte Sound.

ADVENTURE RETURNS

Adventure limped into Queen Charlotte Sound five days after *Resolution* departed. She was storm-battered, her rigging was in shatters and the men were sick and worn down with fatigue. The gales that drove *Resolution* to the south had blown *Adventure* out to sea. Powerful southerly winds then drove them to the north, and Furneaux sought shelter at Tolaga Bay. There they collected fresh water and vegetables but saw no animals, and they left none behind. When the winds shifted, they made for Queen Charlotte Sound in the hope of making the rendezvous with *Resolution*.

Not finding her there, they searched the watering place in Ship Cove and found the sign leading to the corked bottle containing Cook's letter. Planning to catch up with Cook, for the next week the crew and officers busied themselves overhauling *Adventure*, filling the water casks and trading with Māori. When not supervising the workers, Burney trekked around the woods and along the shoreline looking for fresh food for the livestock.[77]

On 12 December 1773, Furneaux recorded an incident that unsettled him. At around 9 a.m. a flotilla of unfamiliar canoes approached the ship. He estimated there were 120 armed warriors in the canoes.[78] When they came alongside *Adventure*, the men tried to climb on board. Furneaux did not like the look of them or the attitude they were displaying, so he only allowed a few men on at a time. When some of the men's behaviour became particularly obnoxious Furneaux ordered them off. The mood of the warriors became ugly which confirmed Furneaux's

fear that they intended taking over his ship. Furneaux wrote that the Māori were 'visibly disappointed in the execution of their grand design, they took to their canoes, all gabbling together in a language, a word of which no one on board could understand.' [79]Alarmed, Furneaux decided it was time to leave the Sound and follow Cook. However, they could not leave without fodder for the animals on *Adventure*. On 17 December, Rowe and another nine men went across to Arapawa Island in a cutter to collect wild greens and grass for the animals. When the men had not returned by the next day, he sent Burney and a contingent of armed marines to look for them. Fannin, the master, went with them.

A Nightmare at Blood Bay

Their search began along the shore of Arapawa Island's East Bay. When they fired their guns to attract the attention of the

Marra, 1775, Plate III. Facing page 94. Sketch presumed to be by the author. Alexander Turnbull Library, R910.4, Cook 1775, Marra Jour, 201

missing men, groups of Māori appeared. They were agitated, some waving spears in a threatening manner, others throwing stones at them. Searching along Arapawa Island's shore, the search party continued to the south. Approaching a small bay to the north of Grass Cove, they saw two Māori men and a dog. When the marines got closer, the men ran off into the woods. Increasingly troubled by the way Māori were acting, the searchers cautiously stepped onto the sand. They discovered part of the missing cutter, along with six shoes and a piece of meat further up the beach. None of the shoes was a pair and one they knew belonged to the Midshipman, Thomas Woodhouse. They assumed the meat was salted beef belonging to the cutter's crew, but then realised it was fresh. Fannin and Burney agreed it must be dog. Māori had pulled seven double canoes onto the stones nearby. They walked towards the canoes and as they got closer saw about twenty sealed flax baskets amongst them. They noticed a dog gnawing on a piece of cooked flesh, which was undoubtedly human.

The horrified men cut open several of the baskets to find roasted remains of their missing people, some of which were still hot.[80] Other baskets, when opened, revealed uncooked body parts that were easily identifiable as belonging to some of *Adventure*'s men. A hand, marked with the letters T. H. and a Tahitian tattoo, belonged to Thomas Hill, one of their crew responsible for the headsails and anchors. Acutely aware of smoke coming from over the hill, Burney ordered the marines back into the boat and they rowed around the point to Grass Cove. On the beach was a large contingent of Māori. Burney estimated there were between 1500 and 2000 people, all in a state of frenzied excitement. Māori called out greetings and made signs for them to land, but as the sailors advanced, those on the beach retreated to the small hill behind them. In shock from the sight of their massacred friends, they fired a bombardment from their grappling gun into the fleeing crowd and scrambled out of the boat in pursuit. A light rain was falling, their muskets became wet and four of the guns misfired.[81] Fearing for their own lives, the men destroyed three canoes that were on the beach, then ran back to their own boat to make their escape. They rowed frantically towards the safety of *Adventure* and her larger guns. While navigating between two small islands to the south of East Bay, they heard someone calling out to them. Burney suspected that at least one man was still alive, hiding amongst the bushes on Arapawa Island. He ordered everyone to be quiet and listen. Silence. They called out several times but there was no reply. Burney later wrote, 'indeed I think it some comfort to reflect that in all probability every man of them must have been killed on the Spot.'[82] They continued rowing, and when they looked back they saw a huge fire 'about three or four miles higher up, which formed a complete oval, reaching from the top of a hill down almost to the water side, the middle space being enclosed all round by the fire, like a hedge.'[83] If a man had evaded the initial massacre, it was unlikely he lived much longer.

Rejoining *Adventure* just before midnight, Burney and the marines carried on board some of the human remains, including two hands, the one belonging to Thomas Hill and the other identified as belonging to John Rowe. Many of the men on *Adventure*

Cook's Voyage in *Resolution,* Having Separated from *Adventure*

wanted to retaliate, but Furneaux saw revenge as futile and dangerous. Given there were probably thousands of Māori in the area, they feverishly prepared *Adventure* and exited Queen Charlotte Sound, leaving some animals behind at Ship Cove. After *Adventure* reached the safety of the Pacific Ocean, the remains of their murdered comrades, wrapped in a hammock weighted with ballast, were committed to the sea.

Furneaux initially followed Cook's route towards the Antarctic. As they sailed closer to Cape Horn, the temperature plummeted. Food was becoming scarce and when they opened some casks of dried peas and flour, they found them inedible. Disheartened, the weather-beaten *Adventure* taking in water, short-handed and the remaining crew freezing and ill, Furneaux ordered Fannin to change course and sail for the Cape of Good Hope. Sometime after they left New Zealand, Fannin scratched over the name 'Grass Cove' on his chart of Cook Strait, replacing it with 'Blood Bay'.[84] *Adventure* brought her shattered crew home to England on 14 July 1774.

RESOLUTION CROSSES THE ANTARCTIC CIRCLE

While Furneaux was fleeing the horrors of Queen Charlotte Sound, Cook was crossing the Antarctic Circle for the second time during this voyage on *Resolution*. As the temperatures dropped to sub-zero, surviving livestock were sheltered below decks. A despondent Johann Forster complained of two-year-old salted meat, served with musty peas, flour and raisins. He was over tempestuous seas, constantly wet decks, rotting timber, and his tiny cabin that was freezing cold and open to the piercing winds. The naturalist was particularly sick of the vile seepage and smells from urinating and defecating animals. In his journal, he moaned that 'everything I touch is moist and mouldy and looks more like a subterraneous mansion for the dead than a habitation for the living.'[85] Forster was not alone in his complaints. Misery settled itself over the ship's crew as *Resolution* rolled and lurched in the large seas. They sailed into showers of hail and sleet. Icicles turned ropes into barbed wire that shredded the seamen's hands.

The naturalists celebrated Christmas by inviting the senior and junior officers, the mates and a few selected others to a special meal. They slaughtered, cooked and served the last hog. There was no such feast for the ordinary seamen who celebrated with salted rations and grog. As they drank to excess, the men appeared deranged to Forster. He likened the scene to an image of hell, with drunken sailors alternately screaming, swearing and praying. Shifting, lurching mountains of ice towering over them heightened the men's fear. *Resolution* could be toppled into the frozen waters at any moment.

On 30 January 1774, they reached the latitude of 71 degrees south. They had gone further south than any person had ever sailed before them. With no livestock left, to celebrate the momentous occasion, Simon Monk, the ship's butcher, killed and roasted Lieutenant Pickersgill's dog.[86] Faced with nothing but solid ice and the deteriorating health of his men, Cook gave up his ambition to find the ever-evasive Southern Continent.

Freezing men complained of severe toothache from drinking freezing water;

rheumatic bones began to swell and throb. Despite the daily rations of wort, many of the men were weak and exhibiting early symptoms of scurvy. The stored oatmeal was rotting and inedible. Rats had broken into rations, eaten some then soaked the rest with urine and faeces. Maggots had also infested the food, 'with the remedy for killing maggots (placing a dead fish atop the infested food, drawing the maggots from the food into the fish) almost as foul as the maggots themselves.' [87] They needed fresh food.

Several grey albatrosses were shot and eaten, but this made little difference to the men's health. Johann took to his bed with a fever. Cook, pale and lean, lost his appetite and had to force himself to eat. As they slowly sailed towards the north, Forster's servant complained of colic and severe pains in his stomach. The doctor gave him purges and a tobacco glyster (an old remedy that involves blowing tobacco smoke into the rectum) and he soon recovered. Cook came down with the same symptoms, the pain becoming so intense he took to his bed. Ship's Surgeon James Patten gave Cook a purge but he vomited; the tobacco glysters did not give him relief either. The captain became so weak he couldn't stand and they feared he would die. In desperation, Patten fed Cook large doses of castor oil. This had the desired effect, and the following day a much-relieved Cook was able to struggle up out of his bed.

More albatrosses were killed and shortly afterwards they became becalmed, their drinking water ran out and they faced death through dehydration. This part of Cook's voyage reflects one of the verses in Coleridge's 'The Rime of the Ancient Mariner'. Coleridge tells of a sailing ship trapped in ice at the South Pole. After escaping, the sailors credit their salvation to an albatross. However, a seaman kills the bird and, when bad luck next strikes the ship, his shipmates, who blame him, hang the albatross's carcass around his neck. The stricken mariner laments:

Alone, alone, all, all alone
Alone on a wide wide sea!
And never a saint took pity on
My soul in agony. [88]

On 5 January a breeze appeared, nudging *Resolution* towards the north. Puffs of wind ruffled the sea, waves appeared and a friendly gale pushed them forward. There are verses in Coleridge's poem that reflect this moment on *Resolution*:

The Sun, right up above the mast,
Had fixed her to the ocean:
But in a minute she 'gan stir,
With a short uneasy motion —
Backwards and forwards half her length
With a short uneasy motion.
Then like a pawing horse let go,
She made a sudden bound:
It flung the blood into my head,
And I fell down in a swound. [89]

There are some subtle links between the 'Rime of the Ancient Mariner' and this voyage: is the prancing horse referring to *Resolution*'s figurehead? Moreover, is it a coincidence that Coleridge published his rhyme in 1798, the same year that Johann Forster died?

Sickness at Sea

In March 1774, despite Cook's preventative measures, scurvy had a strong hold on *Resolution*. Badly affected were Georg Forster and some of the officers. Despite their deteriorating health, the men had to keep the ship going. Some resorted to crawling along the deck to complete their tasks. Now frantic to acquire fresh provisions, Cook altered their course and made for Easter Island (Rapa Nui). The sight of land rewarded them, two days later. Their relief was short-lived as the inhabitants of Easter Island were also starving. Spending just enough time to trade nails and cloth for a few casks of salt water, some sugar cane, bananas and sweet potatoes, they returned to sea.

Increasing the crew's misery were burns and blisters from exposure to the violent noonday sun. Cook's bilious disorder returned, forcing him to take to his bed. Unable to eat the last of the potatoes because of the flatulent effect on his stomach, an emaciated Cook was near death. He hid his symptoms from the men until he was so weak he could barely stand. Then Captain Cook collapsed. James Patten's skill as a surgeon, combined with the generosity of Johann Forster, saved Cook's life. The older Forster was an unpopular man. The seamen frequently ridiculed him and he was often the butt of their jokes. With his constant grumbling and demands, he exasperated Cook and the officers. Forster hated the sea, hated the conditions on board and often found other people's behaviour and proximity intolerable. However, Forster had empathy for the animals on *Resolution*. The sight, sound and smell of livestock slaughtered must have tormented him.

Forster also loved his dogs. Yet, as Cook lay dying from starvation, Johann Forster willingly sacrificed his Tahitian puppy so that Cook might live. The surgeon gave Cook hot bed baths and wrapped his stomach with hot towels. This relaxed Cook's muscles and intestines, allowing his body to purge itself. They killed the puppy and cut its carcass into quarters. Each day they turned one quarter into broth and hand-fed it to Cook. Cook's stomach was able to tolerate the broth, and he gradually recovered. A delighted Johann wrote: 'By such small helps we succeeded in preserving a life upon which the success of the voyage in a great measure depended.'[90] The naturalists also benefited from sacrificing the dog. Sparrman recorded: 'this was also tasted by us with a great benefit to health.'[91]

Pacific Islands' Bounty

On 8 April 1774, *Resolution* reached the Marquesas Islands. With tremendous joy, the exhausted, ravenous sailors swapped nails for fresh breadfruit, bananas, one pig and some casks of fresh water. Two days later, they had acquired another eighteen pigs. On an excursion when they were out buying more, one of the sailors let go a pig and it ran off. The islanders were shocked when Cook struck the sailor for letting it go.[92]

With only enough food to feed them for a week, they steered for the Society Islands. First, they came across a small group of islands connected by a coral reef. Standing on the beach were warriors, each armed with a long spear and a club. Lieutenant Kempe, escorted by some armed marines, cautiously took a small boat to the shore, laden with goods to trade. He returned shortly after with five dogs and information that the woods were full of jittery locals. This breed of dog differed from the Polynesian dog that they generally came across in the Pacific Islands. According to Georg Forster, the 'dogs were in general small and thick, with a large head, not unlike that of our bull dogs.'[93] They were white and covered in a fine, long hair.

They landed in Tahiti a week later, mooring at Matavai Bay. The first thing they noticed was how much improved the village was. The people appeared to be considerably better off economically, with the erection of new houses and most family groups having at least two large hogs. Forster attributed this new wealth to the nails and iron tools they had acquired from the Europeans. Walking past the chief's house, they came across the two goats Furneaux had given to Otoo in August 1773. The older doe was again in kid: 'the She-Goat had soon after kidded, and the 2 kids were now nearly as big as the mother.'[94]

The following day Otoo brought them some hogs. He wanted more hatchets, some red feathers and some more cats. They handed him some cats. The Tahitians now had more than twenty cats.[95] Delighted with the reception they received, Cook decided to stay longer at Matavai so they could complete some much-needed repairs on *Resolution*. He also took the opportunity to put his last nanny goat with the buck given to Otoo by Furneaux.[96]

While *Resolution* was under repair they purchased more pigs. Soon they had so many hogs on board that they did not have enough food to feed them all. Some of these pigs were described as being extremely fat, which suggests they may have been the Chinese breed that existed on the island. Even before they left the port, they found the fat pigs would not eat the food they were offered. Before the animals became too emaciated, they killed them and salted the meat.

Prior to returning to sea, the gentlemen dined on a large bonito (similar to tuna). While these fish were edible, they became toxic if they ate poisonous mangrove fruit.[97]

This was not the gentlemen's lucky day. For days, they suffered with pain throughout their body. In the worst affected, their saliva glands became swollen, 'and discharged an extraordinary quantity of saliva, so that it run out of their mouths involuntarily. In a few a painful erection of the penis was observed, and some even found that their teeth were grown loose.'[98] Some animals also suffered. Someone fed a tame Tahitian parrot a small morsel of the fish, and it died in agony. The dogs that feasted on the bones, fins and entrails of the fish fell violently ill. One dog crawled into a small boat on *Resolution*'s deck where it lay down in some water, paralysed. They threw the suffering dog overboard to shorten its agony. Another dog, equally sick, was given an infusion of tobacco to make it vomit, but it died from the treatment. A hog, which had eaten some of the innards of the fish, also died.[99]

By 11 May 1774, with all essential repairs to *Resolution* complete and the men recovered from the effects of the poisoned fish, they sailed out of Tahiti. From there *Resolution* sailed to other islands in the South Pacific, including Ra'iātea, collecting more dogs and hogs on their way. At Oddidy's request, they left him behind at Ra'iātea. More of the hogs were slaughtered, the meat salted and stored for future consumption.

Six weeks later, on 22 July, they approached the New Hebrides (Vanuatu) island of Malekula. People waded into the sea, coming towards them armed with clubs, bows, arrows and spears. Rather than attacking the ship, however, the islanders wanted to trade some of their weapons, including some blunt arrows pointed with bone. The men suspected a trap when they saw that the points of the arrows were smeared with a black/green residue. As an experiment, Patten wounded a young dog in the leg with one of the dubious spears, to see if it would have a reaction to a poison. The dog showed no negative effects, so they purchased more. They later discovered the substance was a harmless ointment that the islanders believed had magical properties.

They spent the following day on shore cutting down trees and replenishing their casks of fresh water. Some of the men went out in the harbour to catch fish with hooked lines. John Elliott caught two red fish[100] the size of large bream. Some others caught a nine-foot shark, a rockfish and a sucking fish. While preparing the red fish for the officers' and petty officers' dinner, the guts and other waste fragments were fed to some dogs and a pig. That evening everyone who had eaten the red fish became extremely ill. Several had violent vomiting and diarrhoea accompanied by a fever and headache. Others experienced a numbing pain in their arms, knees and legs and had difficulty walking. The dogs suffered similar symptoms to the men while the pig swelled to a great size and died the following day. Fortuitously for the violently ill men, the surgeon was able to see to them as he had dined with Cook and neither had eaten the red fish. More dogs became ill, as the healthy dogs ate what the sick dogs vomited.[101] A pig that had also eaten what the dogs brought up

died. The surgeon opened it up to find 'the liver and intestines were turned quite black.'[102]

After a few days the men and dogs recovered. There were no dogs on Malekula, so Cook presented a young pair, purchased a few months earlier at the Society Islands, to the local people. Before leaving Malekula, Patten subjected a second dog to the substance to determine if the grease on the arrows was poisonous. A cut was made in the thigh of a young dog: 'some of the stuff from the arrow and likewise the green substance were scraped off and put into the wound and then covered with a sticking plaster, in order to keep the supposed poison in the wound; at six o'clock the dog was still well.'[103] Again, the grease proved not to be poisonous and the dog lived to eat and play with the other dogs, only limping a little bit because of the wound.

More islands, more stops and more misunderstandings and skirmishes followed, with nothing relative to animals occurring until 10 August 1774, when they anchored at Tanna (a volcanic island in Vanuatu). Cook invited a local man on board and when he saw the dogs, he called them 'Booga' and asked Cook for some. Cook gave him a dog and a bitch, but based on the following story, these dogs did not survive long enough to reproduce. In 1841 and 1842 the Reverend George Turner worked in Vanuatu. He met an old man from Tanna who claimed to have been present when Cook arrived. The old man was about ten years old when Cook was there. He recalled two 'Tangarooah' being left behind, but said one died soon after *Resolution* left and the other howled so pitifully after its mate, the islanders killed it.[104]

They were nearly two weeks in Tanna, making repairs to *Resolution* amongst the noise and ash from the active volcano. A dignified old man and his son complained to Cook the seamen had started sawing a club wood tree that was hanging over the watering place. The locals had asked the men to stop and they did. Cook paid for the tree with some cloth and a dog when he saw how badly damaged it was. On 20 August the volcano, having been relatively quiet for a few days, spewed huge boulders into the air. Anticipating further eruptions, they left the island for the safety of the open sea.

Loss at New Caledonia

Cook decided it was time to return to New Zealand. Heading on a course south-west of the New Hebrides, on 5 September they came across the long, narrow island now known as New Caledonia. Cook had hoped to collect fresh water and more pigs there; however, when he asked about their animals, he found they had 'no knowledge of goats, hogs, dogs, or cats.'[105] The day after they arrived there, the ship's butcher, Simon Monk, fell down the main hatchway and fractured his skull. He died the following morning. Monk was a great loss, not only because of his skill as a butcher but also because of his character. Johann Forster described Monk as 'a laborious, indefatigable man.'[106] Despite Forster's sacrifice of the Tahitian puppy, his standing with the seamen did not improve. He asked for a boat to take him to the shore. It was not until he sat down to his lunch that Lieutenant Kempe told him the boat was ready. Forster refused to leave until he had finished his meal. When he went on deck, the boat was gone. Some of the crew were standing on the shore laughing with the locals as they scratched the back of a sow.

Forster was trapped on *Resolution* until Cook returned.

Monk's body was committed to the sea. After the ceremony, Cook went for a walk over the hills. While he was gone, his clerk, Alexander Dewar, saw one of the local fishermen catch a large toadfish (a type of pufferfish).[107] Dewar purchased the fish and took it back to the ship. By the time the Forsters had finished describing and drawing the fish, it was too late to be prepared for the gentlemen's tea. Keeping most of the fish for the following day's dinner, the cook fried the liver for Cook, Sparrman and the Forsters' supper. When the fried liver arrived, Cook ate a small piece, Georg ate about half what Cook had and Johann had twice as much as Cook. Sparrman ate none, 'for he never eats any liver of any animal.'[108] An hour after they had completed their supper and were sipping on wine, a distressed servant rushed in and reported that he had left the rest of the liver and the roe of the fish on the bench. Two dogs had jumped up and eaten it and half an hour later, they both became sick and vomited it back up. One of the dogs was the subject of the experiment with the arrow at Malekula.[109] The men laughed at the dogs' exploits and went off to bed.

Johann Forster woke up at about four in the morning feeling giddy, his hands and feet were numb and his stomach felt heavy, as if he had overeaten. When he got up, he reeled like a drunk and could not walk or stand. He called for his servant, who helped him to the toilet. There he passed a bowel motion and threw up the liver. As the liver came up, it burnt and grazed his throat. When he returned to the cabin he shared with Georg, he found his son awake and suffering the same symptoms. With the help of his servant, Johann made his way to the steerage where Sparrman was sleeping. He woke Sparrman up to see if he was also sick. Sparrman was fine but Cook, whose apartment was next to Sparrman's, called out for help. He could neither stand nor walk. They sent for Patten who suggested they take an emetic to induce vomiting. Learning that a little Polynesian pig fed scraps from the fish had died terrified everyone, as Cook's symptoms had worsened. He had lost his sense of feeling and was not able to distinguish between light and heavy objects.[110] For days, the men who had partaken of the fish suffered from gripe, severe aching bones, giddiness and headaches. A rash of pimples appeared on their hands, the skin peeled off their bodies and the secretion of saliva became excessive. The dogs that had fed upon the toadfish were in a worse state, but gradually the two dogs, Cook and the Forsters recovered.

Before leaving New Caledonia, Cook gave the chief an adolescent dog and bitch in trade for sugar cane and yams. 'The dog was red and white, but the bitch was all red, or the colour of an English fox.'[111] Cook gave another man two pigs, a small boar and sow. On 30 September 1774, they entered a small atoll Cook named Botany Island. While there, Lieutenant Kempe caught a fish similar to the one that poisoned Cook and the Forsters. Kempe ordered the fish cleaned, cooked and served to him. His friends talked him out of eating the fish; however, a little dog was not so lucky. The dog, fed the entrails of the fish, spent several days in agony. To end its suffering, they threw it overboard. Ten days later, they sighted Norfolk Island. They stayed there long enough to collect fresh water, some cabbages and grass for the animals, and then steered for New Zealand.

Cook's Fourth Anchorage in Ship Cove

On 18 October Cook anchored for the fourth time in Queen Charlotte Sound. The first thing they did was look for the bottle and note left for Furneaux in November the previous year. There was no corked bottle, suggesting that either *Adventure* had been there or Māori had found it. They knew Furneaux had found the note when they saw some trees chopped down by axes, and some animals, probably pigs and poultry, that belonged to *Adventure*.

Cook was surprised no Māori came to welcome them or to trade. He ordered the gun fired in the evening to attract people living further away, but there was no response. They lit a fire at the pā on Motuara Island, and still no one came to trade. Cook feared warring tribes had attacked and killed local Māori. Some of the crew saw two canoes off the southernmost point of Long Island a week later. They had their sails up, but when they saw *Resolution*, the people took down the sails and furiously paddled back in the direction they had come. This made no sense to Cook. Later that same day, they heard people shouting from the hill on the southern side of Resolution Bay. Taking a small boat, they went in search of them. Seeing a group at the top of the hill, they landed on the beach. Shortly after, one middle-aged man Cook recognised came down the hill to greet them, followed close behind by some others. Georg Forster referred to the middle-aged man as Peeterré.[112] His Māori name was Matahouah, of Ngāi Tahu.[113]

Artist unknown (Author's collection)

Seeing the Europeans to be friendly, other people, most of them strangers, came down to the beach to greet them.

The next day, Matahouah, accompanied by five canoes and a large party of Māori, came to Ship Cove to trade. As they bartered, Cook sensed an unusual nervousness amongst the people. He asked Matahouah if he knew what had become of *Adventure*. According to Matahouah, a ship smashed to pieces on the coast of the North Island during a storm. Cook was unsure if this had been *Adventure*'s fate as there were some inconsistencies to the story. Now convinced *Adventure* had sailed away, the Europeans visited the remote area of West Bay to see if the hogs and poultry they released there had survived. Finding no sign of the animals, or evidence that other people had been there, they decided the animals had retreated into the thickest part of the woods. As they were leaving, one of the Forsters reported hearing what he thought was the squealing of a pig in the woods, quite close to where there were some human habitations. A week later they found confirmation that at least one hen had survived 'for a hen's egg was, some days before, found in the woods almost new laid.[114]'

Evidence that at least one pig had survived reached Cook. Johann Forster was searching for plants on Long Island, when several of the gentlemen accompanying him reported seeing what they agreed was a large black boar on the beach.[115] Cook was delighted, as Furneaux had released their only large black boar in June 1773. He realised that if Māori had not destroyed the boar, it was possible all the animals they gave them had survived. Cook recorded in his journal: 'Since the Natives did not destroy these Hogs when in their possession, we cannot suppose they will attempt it now, so that there is little fear but that this Country will soon be stocked with these Animals, both in a wild and domestic state. I am in doubt that the goats I put ashore are killed, for if they killed the goats why should they not the hogs also.'[116]

Thinking the boar was on his own, Cook decided to catch and put him on the mainland with a sow that was already pregnant. Bad weather interrupted Cook's plans. A group went back to Long Island a few days later, when the weather was calm, the pregnant sow safely secured on the boat. She was to be a companion for the boar. When they came to the area where the boar had been, instead of the boar they found the large black sow released by Furneaux in June 1773. Seeing no advantage in leaving the pregnant sow on the island, they returned her to the ship.

The New Passage

Preparing to leave New Zealand within the next few days, Cook had something else he wanted to explore. Having noticed a rippling tide in the bay, which was otherwise a millpond, Cook was convinced there was another entrance into Queen Charlotte Sound. He decided to take the pinnace and head up to the end of the sound in search of the passage.

On 5 November 1774, accompanied by the Forsters and some marines, they left *Resolution* at eight in the morning. Meeting a canoe coming towards them, they asked the men about a passage to the sea. By pointing, the Māori directed them back to a channel they had already passed. Cook abandoned his plan to go to the southern end of the sound, instead steering towards what would later become Tory Channel (Te Kura Te Au). They discovered inside the narrow entrance a spacious bay. Māori lined both shores. The elderly chief, Te Ringapuhi, greeted Cook when he stepped on shore. Within minutes, over 200 Māori, many of whom were armed, surrounded them. Georg Forster was uncomfortable, exclaiming that there was 'a much greater number than we had suspected the Sound to contain, or had ever seen assembled together.'[117] When the chief confirmed the channel led to the ocean, Cook thought it wise to leave and continue on their excursion. Advancing further up the passage, they glimpsed seabirds. At 4 p.m. they observed waves breaking on rocks at the end of the channel. As they got closer, they saw the narrow outlet into Cook Strait and, through the gap between some huge rocks, they could see the North Island. While tempted to sail around Cape Koamaroo (Koamaru) to return to their ship, the wind and tide were against them. Night was approaching and so they turned the pinnace around to return the way they had come. Looking up the hill to the west, they saw a pā built on a high rock that backed onto Grass Cove. Cook now knew Arapawa was an island.

The seamen returned to the ship around ten in the evening, exhausted and famished. The next morning they awoke to cloudy, gloomy weather. Cook took several men over to Long Island in search of the large black sow. He intended putting her to a boar then releasing her again, but she had returned to the bush. While they were on Long Island, a group of Māori, led by Matahouah (now believed to be the son-in-law of Te Ringapuhi),[118] set up camp near the observation tents in Ship Cove. When Cook returned to the ship, he invited Matahouah to join them for dinner in the Great Cabin. Over dinner, Cook again questioned Matahouah about what had become of Furneaux's men. Matahouah confirmed that *Adventure* had arrived soon after *Resolution* left and had stayed between ten and twenty days. He reassured Cook that they had sailed safely away. Before leaving the ship, Matahouah gave Cook a staff of honour and, in return, Cook gave him a set of European clothes. The chief put on the garments and was so proud of his new appearance that some of Cook's people gave him the nickname 'Pedro'.[119]

On 9 November, they prepared to put to sea, but it began to rain steadily and the winds got up. After the local people had removed their temporary abodes from Ship Cove and paddled away, Cook smuggled a sow and a boar into Little Waikawa Bay, to the north of Cannibal Cove.

At daybreak the following morning, they stood out of the sound, cleared the Two Brothers and steered for Cape Campbell. In the afternoon, observing what they now recognised as the eastern entrance into Queen Charlotte Sound, they went close inshore to see the gap more clearly. Satisfied the sound had two entrances, they continued to the south-east.

Time to Go Home

Being the summer months, it was Cook's intention to continue exploring the Pacific Ocean in search of the ever-elusive Great Southern Land. Early in January 1775, finding no evidence of such a land, Cook decided to sail for home. They steered for Cape Town, crossing the Southern Atlantic and calling into various islands to gather fresh provisions. They sailed for weeks, battered by gales, their sails and rigging failing. Their stale provisions became inedible. The ship's biscuits, inhabited by multitudes of tiny insects, moved of their own accord. Once again, the men were starving. This proved ominous for the remaining animals on board. On the evening of 6 March, one of the two remaining Tahitian sows died. She was with pig and was near to her time of farrowing. Johann Forster suggested there had been foul play: 'there are suspicions that she was killed by the people.'[120] He was equally sceptical when their one remaining goat fell sick 'so that it seems the people are determined not to let a living quadruped on board: and one of

the captain's dogs disappeared some weeks ago.'

Anticipating their arrival at Cape Town, on 16 March 1775, Cook, following the orders of the Admiralty, collected all the logbooks, charts and diaries kept by the officers and petty officers. *Resolution* sailed into Cape Town on 23 March. It was here that Cook learnt of the massacre of *Adventure*'s men at Grass Cove.

On Sunday, 20 July 1775, three years and eighteen days after they left England, and a year and a week after Furneaux, the men on *Resolution* once again stepped on English soil. The only animals left on board, intended as gifts for Queen Charlotte, were three Tahitian dogs, a springbok, one meerkat, two eagles and several small birds from the Cape.[121]

Between the second and third voyages

His second voyage considered a huge success, Cook returned home to Mile End, this time without a ship's goat. He had lost only four men, and just one of them to sickness. The myth of a Great Southern Continent disproved, new lands discovered and charted, Cook became a celebrity. He was presented to King George III at St James Palace. The Admiralty promoted him to Post-Captain (which means his promotion to Captain was formalised and posted in the *London Gazette*) and offered him a position at Greenwich Hospital, a home for the Royal Navy's retired seamen. Cook accepted the position, on the understanding that he was free to go if a better opportunity presented itself. He did not have to wait very long.

Omai, the Ra'iātea man who joined *Adventure* in Tahiti, was to return home. Omai had returned to England with Furneaux and became an immediate sensation in London society. Encouraged by Banks and Solander, people had invited Omai to parties and given him gifts. Omai was given a sword and a suit of armour when he was presented at the Palace. The novelty of Omai's presence soon wore off, though, especially when he demonstrated a fondness for the ladies. King George and Lord Sandwich (the First Lord of the Admiralty and sponsor of Cook's voyages of discovery) decided the Tahitian should return to the Society Islands. This decision coincided with Britain's desire to find a sea route linking the Atlantic and Pacific oceans: the Northwest Passage.

Initially Charles Clerke, now promoted to Captain, was to take Omai to Tahiti, or Ra'iātea if he preferred. *Resolution* was refitted for this purpose. Clerke's opportunity to command the voyage was lost when he was put in prison. Clerke was guarantor for his brother's loans. The brother sailed off to the East Indies, resulting in Clerke going to prison for his debts. On 10 February 1776, Cook wrote to the Admiralty offering to take command of the voyage. When released from prison, Clerke was given charge of the support ship, *Discovery*. Formerly named *Diligence*, this was an eighteen-month-old Whitby-built ship. At 91 feet long, she was the smallest ship on Cook's Pacific voyages.

Endnotes

1 Hoare 1982: 133.

2 Ibid.

3 W. Besant (1894). *Captain Cook.* London: Macmillan & Co: 96.

4 Allan, Ensor & Le Fevre 2004

5 Ibid: 164.

6 Ibid: 150.

7 A. Salmond (2009). *Aphrodite's Island: the European discovery of Tahiti.* Auckland: Viking Penguin: 176.

8 Hoare 1982: 159.

9 Hoare 1982: 192.

10 A. Sparrman (1785). *A Voyage to the Cape of Good Hope: towards the Antarctic polar circle, and round the world: but chiefly into the country of the Hottentots and Caffres, from the year 1772 to 1776.* Translated from the Swedish original. (Vols 1 & 2). London: G.G.J. & J. Robinson: 88

11 Hoare 1982: 186

12 Ibid.

13 A. Sparrman (1953). *A Voyage Round the World with Captain James Cook in H.M.S. Resolution.* Translated by Huldine Beamish & Averil Mackenzie-Grieve. London: Robert Hale Ltd: 6.

14 Ibid: 191.

15 Hoare 1982: 233.

16 Sparrman 1953: 9.

17 J.R. Forster (1778). *Observations made during a voyage round the world, on physical geography, natural history, and ethic philosophy ...* London: Robinson: 190.

18 G. Forster (1777). *A voyage round the world, in His Britannic Majesty's sloop Resolution, commanded by Capt. James Cook, during the years 1772, 3, 4 and 5.* Digital archives and Pacific cultures. Accessed via http://pacific.obdurodon.org/ForsterGeorgComplete.html: 15 April.

19 C.R. Low (1892). *Captain Cook's three voyages round the world. With a sketch of his life.* London: George Routledge & Sons, Ltd: 259.

20 Ibid: 265; 'Be fruitful and multiply'.

21 W. Moore (2015). *The Waterfowl Species of Southern Africa.* Windhoek, Namibia. (Accessed via www.gunsonpegs.com/the-sportsman/part-1-the-waterfowl-species-of-southern-africa).

22 Anderson 1784: 131.

23 G. Forster (1777a). *A voyage round the world, in His Britannic Majesty's sloop Resolution, commanded by Capt. James Cook, during the years 1772, 3, 4 and 5.* Vol. 1.

London: 196.

24   A. Sutherland (2016). *No Ordinary Goat: the story of New Zealand's Arapawa Goats.* Wellington: NZ Arapawa Goat Association: 35.

25   Forster 1777: 20 May 1773.

26   Sparrman 1953: 42.

27   McLynn 2011: 198.

28   H. Mitchell & M.J. Mitchell (2004). *Te Tau Ihu o te Waka: a history of Māori of Nelson and Marlborough.* Vol. 1. Wellington: Huia Publishers: 181.

29   T. Wadsworth (2015). *The spatial distribution of pā in Tōtaranui/Queen Charlotte Sound, New Zealand.* A thesis submitted for the degree of Master of Arts, University of Otago, Dunedin, New Zealand: 29.

30   Villiers 1967: 172.

31   Sutherland 2016: 37.

32   Ibid: 191.

33   Hoare 1982: 292.

34   B. Hooper (1975). *With Captain James Cook in the Antarctic and Pacific: the private journal of James Burney, second lieutenant of the Adventure on Cook's second voyage, 1772–1773.* Canberra: National Library of Australia: 99.

35   Hoare 1982: 297.

36   Possibly Pani, meaning orphan.

37   Anderson 1784: 134.

38   Forster 1777: 273.

39   Ibid 501.

40   Forster 1777a: 501.

41   Hoare 1982: 318.

42   Sparrman 1785: 88.

43   Hoare 1982: 303.

44   Forster 1777: 9 June 1773.

45   Hoare 1982: 310.

46   Ibid: 313.

47   Ibid: 318.

48   Ibid: 318.

49   C. Holmes (1982). *Captain Cook's Final Voyage: the journal of Midshipman George Gilbert.* London: Caliban Books: 120.

50   Salmond 2009: 253.

51   Hoare 1982: 340.

52   Details of the ritual surrounding the human sacrifice can be found in Dame Salmond's (2003) *The Trial of the Cannibal Dog'*, pp. 359–61.

53   Forster 1777a: 206.

54   Ibid.

55   Ibid: 377.

56   J.C. Beaglehole (1974). *The Life of Captain James Cook*. London: Adam & Charles Black: 346.

57   Salmond 2003: 213-214.

58   C.H. Diong (1982). *Population biology and management of the feral pig*. A dissertation submitted to the graduate division of the University of Hawaii in partial fulfilment of the requirements for the degree of Doctor of Philosophy in Zoology.

59   Forster 1778: 130.

60   Allen, Matisoo-Smith & Horsburgh 2001

61   Y.F. Huang, X.W. Shi, Y.P. Zhang (1999 Dec.). 'Mitochondrial genetic variation in Chinese pigs and wild boars', *Biochem Genet.* 37: 11–12, pp. 335–43.

62   Forster 1777: 5 October 1773.

63   Sparrman 1953: 97.

64   Hoare 1982: 406.

65   Forster 1777a: 483.

66   A. Salmond (1997). *Between Worlds: early exchanges between Māori and Europeans 1773–1815*. Auckland: Viking Penguin Books: 87.

67   W. Smith (1842). *The Voyages of Captain James Cook round the world*, Vol. 1. London. https://australianmuseum.net.au/image/endeavour-in-tahiti-1769: 430.

68   Holmes 1982: 164

69   J. Marra (1775). *Journal of the* Resolution's *voyage: in 1772, 1773, 1774, and 1775. On Discovery to the southern hemisphere. Also a journal of the* Adventure's *voyage, in the years 1772, 1773, and 1774. ... Illustrated with a chart, ... and other cuts.* London: Printed for F. Newbery: 78–79.

70   Cook, et al. 1821: 245

71   Low 1892: 175.

72   Marra 1775: 101.

73   Ibid: 100; Hoare 1982: 418.

74   Hoare 1982: 421.

75   Forster 1777a: 507.

76   Hoare: 1982: 426

77   Holmes 1982: 170.

78   G.W. Anderson & W.H.D. Rouse (Ed.). (1906). *Captain Cook's Second Voyage.* London: Blackie & Son Ltd: 41.

79   Ibid

80   W. Bayly (1772–1774). *Manuscript private journal kept by Will Bayly, astronomer to the second voyage of Captain Cook 1772–*

1775. Wellington: Alexander Turnbull Library, National Archives. Ref: fMS-015: 18 December 1773.

81 Anderson 1784: 309.

82 Holmes 1982: 177.

83 Sherrin & Wallace 1890: 53.

84 Beaglehole 1974: 446.

85 Hoare 1982: 438

86 Marra 1775: 127.

87 M. Dugard (2001). *Farther Than Any Man. The rise and fall of Captain James Cook*. Australia: Allen & Unwin: 27.

88 S.T. Coleridge (1866). *The Rime of the Ancient Mariner. Illustrated.* London: D. Appleton & Co: 27.

89 Ibid: 34–35.

90 G. Forster (1777b). *A voyage round the world, in His Britannic Majesty's sloop Resolution, commanded by Capt. James Cook, during the years 1772, 3, 4 and 5.* Vol. 2. London: 3.

91 Sparrman 1953: 113.

92 Hoare 1982: 488.

93 Marra 1775: 170.

94 Hoare 1982: 497.

95 E. Rhys (1906). *Captain Cook's Voyages of Discovery.* London: J.M. Dent & Sons Ltd: 174.

96 Hoare 1982: 652.

97 Sparrman 1953: 139.

98 Ibid: 646.

99 Ibid: 647.

100 It is likely the fish were not a poisonous species, rather they were contaminated by ciguatoxins. Ciguatera fish poisoning is found in tropical locations such as the Pacific Ocean, and can affect any reef fish, including red snapper, hog fish, kingfish, etc. The poison is concentrated in the liver, roe, intestines and head of the fish.

101 Sparrman 1953: 571.

102 Marra 1775: 264.

103 Ibid: 575.

104 G. Turner (1861). *Nineteen Years in Polynesia: missionary life, travels and researches in the islands of the Pacific.* Paternoster Row, London: John Snow: 87.

105 Rhys 1906: 194.

106 Hoare 1982: 646.

107 Ibid: 649.

108 Ibid.

109   Ibid: 244.

110   Anderson 1784: 176.

111   Rhys 1906: 196.

112   Forster 1777b: 455.

113   Salmond 1997: 110.

114   Ibid: 8 November 1774.

115   Hoare 1982: 677.

116   J.C. Beaglehole (Ed.). (1961). *The Journals of Captain James Cook on his Voyages of Discovery*. Vol. 2: The voyage of Resolution and Adventure 1772–1775. London: Routledge Francis Taylor & Group: 573.

117   Forster 1777b: 472.

118   Mitchell & Mitchell 2004: 191.

119   J. Cook & J. King (1785). *A voyage to the Pacific Ocean for making discoveries in the northern hemisphere: performed under the direction of Captains Cook, Clerke, and Gore, in the years 1776, 1777, 1778, 1779, 1780*. In three volumes. London: Published by order of the Lords Commissioners of the Admiralty: 67.

120   Hoare 1982: 727.

121   J.C. Beaglehole (Ed.). (1961). *The Journals of Captain James Cook on his Voyages of Discovery. Vol. 2: The voyage of* Resolution and Adventure 1772–1775. London: Routledge Francis Taylor & Group: 959.

PART THREE

COOK'S FINAL VOYAGE

Cook's Third Voyage, Accompanied by *Discovery*

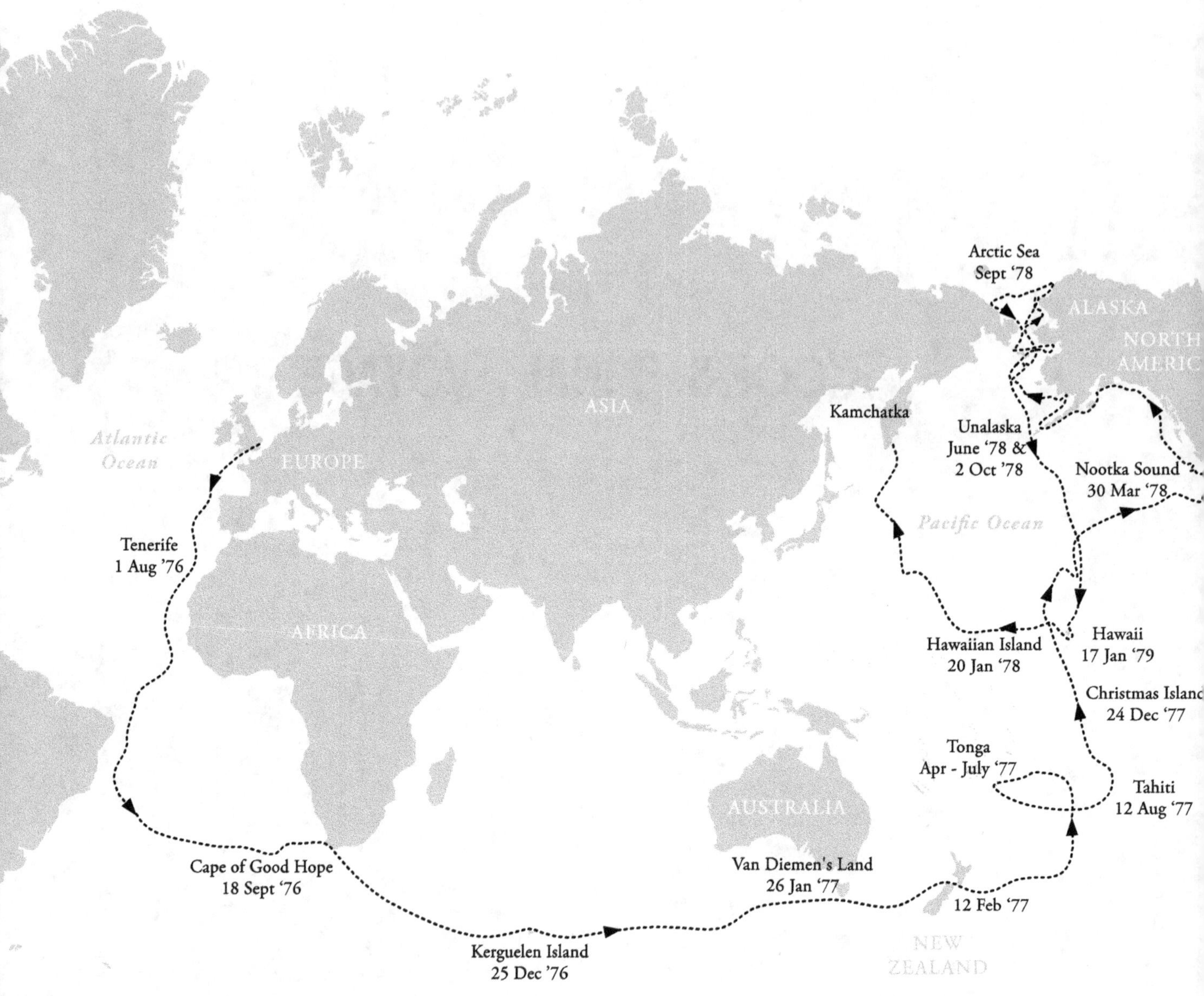

The stories of animals that sailed on Cook's voyages ends at Kamchatka. Resolution and Discovery eventually return to England, entering the Thames on 4 Oct '80.

Chapter 5

PREPARATIONS

The Ships' Company

At least four men on this voyage had sailed with Cook on the two earlier voyages. Clerke was the only officer on all three of Cook's voyages to the South Pacific. The other three were: William Harvey, a midshipman on *Resolution*; John Ramsay, who had been cook on *Resolution* during the second voyage and was now an able seaman; and Samuel Gibson, a private who had deserted at Tahiti on the *Endeavour*, who was a Corporal of Marines on *Resolution* during the second voyage and would now be Sergeant of Marines on *Resolution*. Cook's First Lieutenant was American-born John Gore. This was to be John Gore's third voyage around the world. He had sailed on *Dolphin*, was Third Lieutenant on *Endeavour*, and the man who shot a kangaroo in Australia then shared it with his mates rather than hand it over to Banks. Another familiar name from Cook's previous voyages was William Anderson. Anderson had been Surgeon's Mate on *Resolution* and was the Surgeon on this voyage. His assistants were David Samwell and William Ellis. The Master on *Resolution* was William Bligh, twenty-one years old. Lord Sandwich recommended

Bligh for the voyage. In all, there were 112 men on *Resolution*.

Sailing on *Discovery* under Clerke were seventy-two men. Clerke's First Lieutenant was James Burney. Burney had been Second Lieutenant on *Adventure* and the man who found the remains of the missing men following the massacre at Grass Cove. Clerke's Second Lieutenant was John Rickman. The Master on *Discovery* was Thomas Edgar and the artist for the voyage was John Webber, twenty-four years old. William Bayly had been the astronomer on *Adventure* and that was his role on this voyage.

The Orders

Cook received three orders for this expedition: to find the Northwest Passage between the Pacific Ocean and the Northern Sea; to return Omai home to Tahiti, or Ra'iātea if that was his preference; and to distribute livestock amongst the South Pacific islands. The last order was recommended by King George III, known as 'Farmer George', who was determined that Māori and the neighbouring Pacific Islanders would receive the benefits of British livestock. Ready to be loaded on board *Resolution* and *Discovery* at Cook's discretion were a selection of farm animals gifted by King George, as well as animals for Omai supplied by Lord Sandwich. Because *Resolution* was the larger of the two ships, she was the one equipped to carry most of the livestock. The temporary enclosures contained sixteen English sheep, rabbits, a large number of sows and several hogs, two cows with their calves and a bull, as well as goats, a peacock and a peahen.

In addition to the king's gifts and Omai's animals, added to the menagerie were livestock for the journey, the animals brought on board by the sailors and officers: nanny goats for their milk, pet dogs and cats, as well as hens for eggs. To be fitted into a relatively small ship already crammed with men and provisions for a voyage to the other side of the world were animals, their pens, cages, bedding, food and water.

Cook's Ark, in the style of Kennaway, by Lex McKay, ©2018

Chapter 6

COOK'S THIRD CIRCUMNAVIGATION

RESOLUTION SAILS ALONE

Cook left England on 12 July 1776 on what would prove to be his final voyage. Ironically, his crew believed the date to be lucky because it was the same day and month *Resolution* had sailed out of Plymouth on her first circumnavigation. Clerke, delayed by the bailiffs due to his brother's debts, would follow later on *Discovery*. Cook instructed Clerke to follow him to St Jago at the Cape Verde Islands. If delayed, Clerke would rendezvous with Cook at the Cape of Good Hope. All the king's animals were loaded onto *Resolution* because of the uncertainty as to when *Discovery* would sail.

Poor workmanship on *Resolution*'s repairs hampered Cook's third voyage. Rainwater saturated the forward sail room and the storeroom in the first rough weather they encountered. As they sailed into the Bay of Biscay, a storm damaged the stored hay and corn meant for the animals.[1] The voyage continued towards the Canary Islands following temporary repairs made to *Resolution*. On 1 August, *Resolution* arrived at Tenerife. They stopped there for three days, which gave the men some respite. The sailors went on shore while the stock remained penned on the ship. Supplies refilled, including fresh food, water and brandy, they returned to sea. Intending to berth at the Cape Verde Islands and wait for Clerke, because of the weather they only stopped long enough to pick up a few provisions, including some goats, then continued on to Cape Town, arriving there on 18 September 1776.

CLERKE LEAVES ENGLAND

By the time Cook left the Cape Verde Islands, Clerke had already left England on *Discovery*. She sailed in relative calm for a week, then the skies darkened and the ocean began to rise and break. Within hours, Clerke was fighting an electrical storm. It was so severe that experienced seamen and novice sailors feared for their lives.[2] Surviving the storm, they called in at Porto Praya in the Cape Verde Islands. On learning *Resolution* wasn't there, Clerke ordered they leave the bay on the same day. In their urgency to catch up with Cook, they neglected the traditional mariner's rite-of-passage ceremony of dunking when crossing the equator.

THE CAPE

While Clerke was battling the storms and the hardships common to a long sea voyage, Cook anchored at Cape Town in the shadow of Table Mountain. With *Resolution* safely moored, the men established a camp on shore. Cape Town's Lieutenant Governor gave Cook permission to unload the livestock so they could recover from the voyage. The bull, two cows and their calves went inland to graze alongside some African livestock. Sixteen English sheep were also unloaded, but Cook was concerned about the interest shown in them. He kept them close by their tents during the day and had them penned each night. One night, some rogue dogs got amongst the sheep, killing four and scattering the rest. Cook suspected the dogs were a ruse to separate the sheep so others could carry them off. They employed some shifty-looking locals to help find them and recovered all but two ewes and a ram. Another ram, savaged by the dogs, was only good for the table. The Cape's Lieutenant Governor recompensed their loss by offering Cook one of his valuable Spanish rams. Cooked thanked the man for his generosity, and instead purchased some of the Cape's fat-tailed breed.[3] For the South Pacific Islands, Cook required quantity, not quality.

Rendezvous at Cape Town

Discovery arrived at Cape Town on 10 November 1776. As they entered Table Bay, Clerke saluted the fort with thirteen guns. The fort responded with thirteen blasts, followed closely by *Resolution*'s welcome salute of nine guns. Cook was elated to see his support ship. Eager to continue the journey, he ordered all hands be engaged in repairing *Discovery*. Soon after they went on shore, Lieutenant Rickman expressed frustration that they had to travel inland to find fresh supplies: 'all sorts of provision, of

beef, mutton, poultry, flour, butter, cheese and every other necessary, is brought from four to five and twenty days' journey from Cape Town.[4] They were ready to leave by the end of November. Their last task was to acquire and load more animals. They purchased livestock as fresh meat for the journey ahead, as well as four horses (two young colts and two mares) 'of a delicate breed'. Omai, who had learnt to ride when he was in London, hoped the horses were for him. How impressed his people would be when they saw him riding these exotic creatures. Cook had the four horses stabled together in Omai's small cabin, much to his delight. Cook, in what would be his final letter to Lord Sandwich dated 26 November 1776, wrote: 'The taking on board of some horses has made Omai completely happy, he consented with raptures to give up his cabin to make room for them.'

Also purchased were two young bulls and two heifers of the horned variety, and some more African rams and ewes. Added to the list were some female dogs, some with a litter of puppies. According to Ledyard, they also put on *Resolution*: twenty Cape Town goats, some monkeys, ducks, geese, turkeys, peacocks, hares, rabbits and some more cats. 'Stored with these, the *Resolution* resembled the Ark, in which pairs of all the animals that were to stock the earth were collected; and with their [food], they occupied no small part of the ship's stowage.'[5] The total number of animals they had on board both ships is unclear, although Midshipman George Gilbert provides us with an estimate of those on *Resolution*. As well as the English bull, two English cows and their calves, some English goats and the six English sheep they recovered after the dog attack, 'We likewise carried with us two Horses, two Mares. Three Bulls, four Cows, two Calves, fifteen goats, 30 Sheep, a peacock and hen, Turkeys, Rabbits, Geese, Ducks and Fowls in great plenty.'[6] Omitted from Gilbert's list are the ship's milking goats, cats and rats. On seeing all the animals, Cook added to his letter to Lord Sandwich: 'Nothing is wanting but a few females of our own species to make the Resolution a complete ark, for I have taken the liberty to add considerably to the number of animals your Lordship was pleased to order to be put on board in England: as my intention for so doing is for the good of posterity, I have no doubt but it will meet with your Lordships approbation.'[7]

From Cape Town to New Zealand

The two ships left the Cape together on 2 December. Men tended the animals on *Resolution* around the clock. Soon after leaving Table Bay, they fell into tempestuous weather. Tightly packed together, smaller animals were relatively safe in their pens. Larger animals had to have their movements restricted to stop them being bashed to death against the timber. Cattle were put in slings to protect their legs from being broken, and their heads secured to stop them being knocked against the side of the stall. Hides from slaughtered animals were wrapped around them to prevent bruising. When the seas calmed, the animals were released from their restrictions. One by one they would be carefully walked around the top deck for exercise. For three weeks the voyagers struggled against moody seas, sometimes fighting gales and huge swells. At other times they were becalmed and unable to see through the thick fog. Most of the animals not meant for the table survived the voyage so far, as they were not exposed to the freezing conditions of the Antarctic waters.

On Christmas Eve they anchored near a group of small uncharted islands. Here they were able to get fresh water, as well as seal blubber they could convert to oil. While combing the beach, one of the seamen saw a sealed glass bottle suspended by a wire between two rocks. The man took the bottle to Cook who uncorked it. Written in French and Latin was a note from Yves-Joseph de Kerguelen, dated four years earlier. He had discovered and claimed the islands for France, naming them Kerguelen, after himself. Ellis, the assistant surgeon, had his own name for the barren island that had no trees or palatable greens: The Island of Desolation.

Cook put the note back in the bottle, along with a silver two-penny coin dated 1772, and sealed it with a leaden cap. The bottle was left on a pile of stones for the next explorers to find. Cook then sent some men to fill the casks with water, and some others to gather the island's coarse grass for the starving stock. Shortly after they returned to sea some of the animals became ill. Their muscles hardened and their bodies swelled to an alarming size. Two young bulls, one heifer, two rams, and several goats died.[8] Cook concluded that something poisonous had been brought on board with the Kerguelen grass. He ordered every last fragment of the grass be thrown overboard. Further investigation revealed the grass given to the affected animals had been taken from a spot on the island where a large number of penguins had been sitting. The grass and the land around this area was

Ellis, William Wade. (1776). *Christmas Harbour, in the Island of Desolation or Kerguelan's [i.e. Kerguelen] Land.* http://nla.gov.au/nla.obj-134490944

heavily polluted with the penguins' dung, but still the seamen had collected it and fed it to the animals. On 30 December they left the Kerguelen Islands and continued their eastward course for New Zealand.

On 14 January 1777 a hurricane developed and when the winds died down, a thick grey fog shrouded them. The fog was so dense that the ships continuously rung their bells and fired their guns to avoid crashing into each other. Then a cyclone struck, buffeting the ships for five days. Most of the bucks died, followed closely by four does and all the kids born on board or purchased at the Cape. Soon after, two rams, two young bulls and a heifer also died.

Cook sought refuge in Tasmania's Frederick Henry Bay. Having anchored there for three days, they were approached by a group of Aboriginals: eight men and a boy. Amongst other presents, Cook gave them a pair of pigs. 'I had brought two pigs ashore with a view to leave them in the woods. The instant these came within their reach, they seized them, as a dog would have done, by the ears, and were for carrying them immediately with no other intention, as we could perceive, but to kill them.'[9] Omai fired a musket at the Australians which gave them such a fright they dropped the pigs and ran off into the woods. Cook ordered the boar and sow be carried to the end of the bay where they were released a mile into the thick woods, alongside a freshwater stream. He instructed the men to collect fresh grass for the stock but insisted on checking the quality of the pasture as they worked. While the seamen were occupied, the surgeon, Anderson, spent the days scouring the countryside. He returned with a small animal about twice the size of a large rat, which he described as being 'of a dusky colour above, tinged with a brown or rusty cast, and whitish below. About a third of the tail towards its tip is white, and bare underneath, by which it probably hangs on the branches of trees in its search for berries.'[10] In all probability Anderson had found a brushtail possum (*Trichosurus vulpecula*). He shot it while it was running up a tree like a squirrel.[11] The officers continued excursions inland, fishing the lagoons and discovering varieties of snakes and lizards.

On 28 January, ten unarmed Aboriginals, naked except for animal skins secured to the soles of their feet, came out of the woods and approached a marine. The man was terrified and called out to his mates for help. Omai demonstrated the power of his musket and the Aboriginals left. A larger group of about twenty men arrived the next day. Cook welcomed them with an offering of beads and medals, but they seemed indifferent to the gifts. Except for one extremely inquisitive man. According to David Samwell, the surgeon on *Discovery*, he was 'a little deformed humped-backed fellow'[12] who expressed the greatest joy by laughing, shouting and jumping, when Omai draped a piece of white cloth over his shoulders. Seeing the man's delight, a dozen women joined the group, some of them carrying children on their back cradled in the skin of an animal. The women stayed for about an hour before disappearing back into the woods. The men stayed long enough to help push the boat off the beach.

Once they had sufficient fresh water and greens on board, they sailed out of Tasmania and steered for New Zealand.

WARY RETURN TO QUEEN CHARLOTTE SOUND

On 12 February, less than two weeks after leaving Tasmania, they sailed into Queen Charlotte Sound. But this was a different, cautious crew landing in New Zealand. It was necessary to refresh the men and livestock, and repair the ships, but the men were wary. Every man would have known about the massacre of Furneaux's men in December 1773, and the slaughter following the death of Marion du Fresne and his men at the Bay of Islands in 1772. Shortly after they anchored at Ship Cove, several canoes cautiously approached, waving something white backwards and forwards. The seamen ignored their Māori visitors. All hands remained engaged in unloading stores, digging trenches, erecting the tents and building enclosures for the animals.

Reed & Clark 1956: 5

Omai, who had been present when the men's remains were brought back to *Adventure*, stood silently alongside Cook on the quarterdeck of *Resolution*. As the Māori manoeuvred their canoes closer to the ships, Cook invited them on board. None would climb onto *Resolution*, not even a man who Cook had befriended the last time they were there. Cook wrote, 'Yet now, neither professions of friendship nor presents would prevail upon him to come into the ship.'[13] However, when it became clear that Cook was not seeking vengeance for the deaths of Furneaux's men, trading commenced.

All activity stopped when the animals were disembarked from *Resolution*. The ship was nudged close to the shore. Every man from the two ships — over 180 people — worked to transport the animals from *Resolution* to the safety of Ship Cove. Smaller animals, some in pens, some tethered, were carried to the beach in the boats. Animals too large for the men to handle in the small boats were pushed over the side. Men with prods were arranged in the water to create a channel to the beach. The terrified animals were coaxed to swim to the shore. As the scene unfolded the Māori watched in awe. Samwell recorded: 'Today our ship, which for the variety of living things she contained might be called a second Noah's Ark, poured out the Horses, Cattle, Sheep, goats, etc. with peacocks, Turkeys, Geese and Ducks, to the great Astonishment of the New Zealanders who had never seen Horses or Horned Cattle before.'[14] When the saturated animals scrambled to the safety of the beach, men were positioned to herd them into the purpose-built enclosures. Some, like the cats, dogs and the ships' goats, were free to wander amongst the tents.

With little edible grass growing in Ship Cove, a boat was sent out to collect fresh food for the animals. No longer trusting the Māori's

Webber, John 1751-1793: View in Queen Charlotte's Sound, New Zealand / J. Webber fecit. R.A. - London; Boydell, 1809. Ref: B-098-015. Alexander Turnbull Library, Wellington, New Zealand.

intentions, Cook took some precautions. He appointed a guard of ten marines to protect them when they were on shore. Workmen were ordered to have arms close at hand and when any of them went out in the boats, they were to be accompanied by armed marines and two or three petty officers.

More and more Māori came to trade, but instead of going off to their various habitations, they set up camp close to the sailors, until 'there was not a spot in the cove where a hut could be put up that was not occupied by them, except the place where we had fixed our little encampment.'[15]

Ship Cove soon became a little village, verging on domesticity. Children ran around playing while their elders participated in a variety of activities alongside the sailors. Men and women mixed, and in some cases formed an attachment. One young couple that fell in love was a fourteen-year-old Māori girl, Ghowannahe (her Māori name was probably Anahe, as in Ko Anahe)[16] and one of the young seaman from *Discovery*. His name is not revealed in the manuscripts, but given the emphasis on his youth, and that Clerke was fond of the boy, our Romeo may have been sixteen-year-old Alexander Mouat. Anderson wrote, 'What time he could spare, he generally retired with her, and they spent the day, but oftener the night, in a kind of silent conversation, in which, though words were wanting, their meaning was perfectly understood.'[17] The lad had himself tattooed from head to foot by a Māori tattooist so that soon it was hard to differentiate between him and Māori men.

Still more Māori came, most of them strangers and some only staying for short periods. One latecomer was the chief,

Kahura (of the Rangitāne tribe).[18] Kahura was rumoured to have executed the massacre, and the person who struck the first blow, killing John Rowe, the Master's Mate on *Adventure*. Ellis was present when Kahura came face to face with Cook. 'At first he was very shy, and would not venture on board, fearful no doubt that we should revenge the death of our people upon him; but when he found we took no notice of it, he laid aside that diffidence, and readily came to the ships.'[19]

Some sailors and officers approached Cook, demanding retaliation for the massacre of Furneaux's men. Some friendly Māori who pestered him to punish Kahura supported their petition. Cook refused to do so, explaining: 'if I had followed the advice of all our pretended friends, I might have extirpated the whole race; for the people of each hamlet or village, by turns, applied to me to destroy the other.'[20]

Frustrated with Cook's leniency towards the cannibals, some of the men on *Discovery* took their anger out on a New Zealand dog. In her book *The Trial of the Cannibal Dog*, Dame Anne Salmond[21] acknowledges the extreme resentment felt by the men who had been on *Adventure*, including Omai and Burney. To release the tension, one of the crew acquired a dog from Kahura's people. In a perverted sort of justice for their dead comrades, some of the seamen held a mock court martial where it was determined the dog, being of cannibal origin, should be executed. They found the dog guilty and promptly killed, cooked and ate it.

The two captains explored Queen Charlotte Sound while the crew prepared the ships for the next part of the voyage. On 16 February Cook and Clerke took the pinnace and some of the longboats to Grass Cove. As they approached the beach, Cook's old friend, Matahouah (known to the crews as Pedro) was waiting, along with several armed and clearly agitated warriors. Using Omai as translator, Cook informed Matahouah he knew of the massacre and asked him what motivated the killing of the seamen. Matahouah's version of the tragedy was similar to what Cook had already heard. Cook determined the disastrous incident had arisen over an unpremeditated quarrel between Furneaux's men and Māori.

Preparing to Leave New Zealand

The longboats were loaded with fresh grass and, towards evening, the Europeans headed back towards Ship Cove. As the flotilla moved along the coastline of Arapawa Island, the pinnace slipped quietly into East Bay. Checking there were no Māori around, they rowed silently to the shore. In the near dark, the men removed bundles lying in the bottom of the boat. They carried them onto the beach and into the thick scrub. There, Cook released two ewes and a ram. As to what breed of sheep these were is uncertain, other than that they were probably of English or South African origin. If they were an old English breed, they could have been any of the sheep breeds common at the time, possibly Teeswater, Leicester, Devonshire, Exmoor or Heath if their wool was long, or Dorsetshire, South Down, Hereford, Cheviot, Norfolk, Sussex or Shetland if their wool was short.[22]

Alternatively, if their origins were South African, it is reasonable to assume they were the common fat-tailed breed that were popular at the Cape. They may also have been a breed

of sheep that Banks described on the first voyage. These were a long-legged, tall animal with short horns. They had pendent ears, wattles on the neck, and short hair instead of wool that is generally associated with sheep. Sometime after liberating the sheep, Gilbert, Midshipman on *Resolution*, recorded Cook leaving another two pigs in Queen Charlotte Sound, this time on Motuara Island.[23] These were most likely English pigs as there is no mention of them purchasing African pigs at the Cape on Cook's final voyage.

Collecting and storing grass and celery for the animals kept the crew occupied for several more days, but violent storms delayed their preparations for leaving. When the weather settled an unknown tribe, consisting of about thirty people, came from the upper part of the sound to visit them. Their chief was Tomatongeauooranua[24] (possibly Tamatangi-Au-Uranui[25] or Ko Matongeauoo-ranui). By this time, according to Anderson, 'upwards of two-thirds of the natives of Queen Charlotte's Sound had settled near us.'[26] Then numerous canoes, each containing ninety to a hundred people, arrived from the north. They came on the pretence of trading but, unlike the local Māori, these weren't fishermen. Cook was suspicious of their intentions, as they carried implements and tools easily converted into weapons. Surrounded by Māori of various tribes, unsure of their objective, Cook became nervous. He knew the attack on Furneaux's men occurred as they were preparing to leave, so he decided to keep the time of their departure a secret.

The livestock were in excellent condition and strong enough to continue the voyage. Vast quantities of grass and herbs were now

Norfolk breed (above); Hertfordshire breed (below). Rees 1820: 64

Common sheep (above) and Improved South Down Polled sheep; Rees 1820: 62

stowed on board both ships. Cook gave the order for the turkeys, geese, peacocks, horses, cattle, remaining goats and sheep to be loaded onto *Resolution* and *Discovery*. Māori would know they were about to leave, but they did not know when. The command came at four in the morning on 23 February 1777. The officers roused the men, the tents were pulled down, and the last of their belongings piled into boats and taken to the ships. The masters called to raise the anchors. They did not get far as the tide was against them.

Forced to anchor between Long and Motuara islands, they waited for a favourable wind to take them out to the strait. Cook chose this time to release two pairs of rabbits onto Motuara Island.[27] The origins of these rabbits is unclear. In July 1776, King George III gave Cook some English-bred rabbits. Cook purchased more rabbits at Cape Town in November 1776, and kittens were born during the voyage. Therefore, it is probable they were either an English or South African breed, or a combination of both. If English, they may have been related to the wild English rabbit or the domestic rabbit. If African, it is possible they were a species of European rabbit (*Oryctolagus cuniculus* or common rabbit) that was introduced into the South-west Cape of Africa in the seventeenth century.[28]

Realising the Europeans were leaving, a large contingent of Māori, led by Matahouah, surrounded the ships and clambered aboard. Hundreds of tense Māori, men and women, swarmed the ships. Thinking it prudent to humour their agitated visitors, at the chiefs' request Cook reluctantly gave Matahouah a pregnant doe and a buck. To the other chief, Tomatongeauooranua, he gave a boar and a

sow. The chiefs appeared satisfied with these gifts, making a promise that the animals would be protected and not killed. They instructed their people to withdraw.

Cook and Clerke were now anxious to leave the sound, but the wind continued to be uncooperative. The next day, again Māori approached *Resolution* to trade. Kahura was amongst them and asked to meet with Cook. Knowing Kahura had been involved in the massacre, an irate Omai escorted him into the Great Cabin, demanding, 'There is Kahoora, kill him.'[29] Cook did not kill the man, instead he listened to his version of what had occurred, which matched what he already knew. Still believing the deaths were in retaliation for a perceived injustice, at Kahura's request Cook allowed Webber to sketch a likeness of him. A delighted Kahura sat for Webber in Cook's Great Cabin. He left *Resolution*, but not before sauntering past Omai with a smug look on his face.

At last the wind was in their favour. On 25 February the captains followed the customary procedure by ordering their crews on deck for a roll call. During the muster on *Discovery*, they discovered Ghowannahe's young sailor was missing. However, the surgeon reported the lad was ill and he had sent him to the sick bay. With all seamen accounted for, Cook and Clerke ordered the ships taken out to the strait.

Later that afternoon, when Clerke and his officers were dining on *Resolution*, one of the youth's messmates went to check on him. The lad, his bag, baggage and chest were gone. Prearranged with his girlfriend, he had slipped ashore concealed amongst the crowds of departing Māori. A messenger was immediately dispatched to *Resolution* to ask how to proceed. When they were informed of the missing seaman, the captains and officers were having a few drinks and were inclined to just leave him behind. But Cook was concerned the young adventurer's antics might set a bad precedent for the other men. He sent the sailor's friend, some officers and a boatload of marines back to Ship Cove in search of him. Rickman, who was one of the officers sent to find the pair, wrote: 'It was midnight before the cutter could reach the landing place, and near two in the morning before the marines could find the spot where the lovers used to meet.'[30] There they found the young couple sound asleep. 'Their parting was tender, and for a British sailor and a savage Zealander was not unaffecting.'[31]

Taken to *Resolution* to be tried for desertion, the distressed youth told Cook the idea of deserting came when he was on an excursion with Captain Clerke around the sound. Seeing European sheep, hogs, goats and fowl, sufficient to stock a large plantation,[32] he formed a plan to stay in New Zealand and establish an empire. When Cook asked him if he had not feared for his life, living amongst Māori, he explained that Ghowannahe had assured him he was quite safe. He had asked her about the massacre and she told him that the old man, Goubiah, realising *Adventure* was being prepared to depart, went up into the hill country and invited the warriors to come down and kill the seamen. At first they refused, saying they were friends of the Europeans. Goubiah convinced them the Europeans were cruel enemies, showing them marks and bruises he claimed to have received when they chained him up. Then they said they feared the muskets and the ship's guns. Goubiah told

them not to worry as the sailors would be going to Grass Cove to collect grass for their animals. He said when they gathered grass, they left their guns back at the ship or were careless and left them on the ground while they worked. He also told them that the muskets could be rendered useless if water was thrown over them.

While Ghowannahe would only have been about nine years old at the time of the massacre, she was present at the feast and was able to provide some details about what happened. The youth shared her story with Cook. Goubiah had led them to Grass Cove, where Māori waited, hidden amongst the bush. When the sailors were busy cutting the grass, their guns at a distance, the warriors attacked and killed them. The women made the fires while the men cut the dead men into pieces.[33]

Anderson believed Ghowannahe's account, connecting it to the arrival of the large groups of Māori from the north. Cook listened to this new version of the massacre, then sent the lad back to *Discovery* to receive his punishment of twelve lashes. He does not say which version he believes is true, but a new note creeps into Cook's journal when he left Queen Charlotte Sound for the last time. His attitude towards Māori shifted. Cook had described Māori as 'brave, noble, and open', insisting that 'they are not more wicked than other men.' He now wrote about their cruelty in warfare, saying that they 'kill every soul that falls in their way, not even sparing the Women and Children, and then either feast and gorge themselves on the spot or carry off as many of the dead as they can and do it at home with acts of brutality horrible to relate.'[34] This shift in Cook's attitude towards Māori has a variety of possible causes, including loss of hope, increased cynicism, and familiarity breeding contempt. However, Dame Anne Salmond suggests it was more likely to have arisen from an awareness of having been hoodwinked. When Cook heard Ghowannahe's story, it is likely he felt a fool. He had believed the lies and allowed the death of men under his command to go unpunished. Such a betrayal would have altered Cook's perception of the 'noble savage' and subsequently resulted in a negative impact on any future relationships, not only with Māori but also with Pacific Islanders. This shift in his temperament became apparent shortly after leaving Queen Charlotte Sound.

Cook's nature was passionate, but his temper was usually well-controlled. However, towards the end of the third voyage he gave way more often to his anger and berated his officers and men, shouting and cursing and stamping his feet on the quarterdeck.[35]

If the New Zealanders had lied about what happened to Furneaux's men, why would they not also have lied about the survival of the animals released in the sound? *Discovery*'s young adventurer had claimed there were European animals roaming free in the various bays. When they gave gifts to Māori, they would quickly take them away, offload them somewhere, return, and ask for more. More often than not, more gifts were handed over. Perhaps enough livestock were given to Māori, sufficient to establish a small kingdom? Certainly our young adventurer, who was there, believed so.

Cook soon received evidence that some animals he had introduced into Queen Charlotte Sound survived. As Cook navigated out of New Zealand for the last

time, on board *Resolution* were two Māori boys: 'the oldest called Tiberua was about seventeen years old; the youngest Kohaw was about ten.'[36] The boys, who Salmond identifies as Te Weherua, a chief's son, and Koa,[37] were sailing with Cook as servants to Omai. During the voyage the youths told Cook, some of the animals that he and Furneaux had left in the sound were still alive. They told him Tiratou, the chief who usually resided on Motuara Island and who had helped Cook retrieve some stolen items early in November 1773, had in his possession many cocks and hens, as well as a sow.[38] Cook left knowing that he had achieved his goal to introduce livestock into New Zealand, and that poultry were there in abundance. He intended to do the same in the Pacific Islands.

Tiberua proved to be an intelligent young man who quickly gained the respect of the seamen. Some of his stories so intrigued Cook that he recorded them. Acknowledging that he had not seen it himself, Tiberua confirmed the story told to Cook in 1773, of a ship landing at Terrawitte prior to Endeavour's arrival. He added to this account the story of an animal given to Māori. Cook believed the boy and wrote: 'Taweiharooa told us, their country was indebted to her people for the present of an animal, which they left behind them.'[39] They asked Tiberua to describe the animal, but as he hadn't seen it himself, they could not identify the species. As Tiberua and other Māori had seen a variety of animals at Ship Cove, it is reasonable to suppose that none of these types were the mystery animal. Is there a connection between this unknown animal (that Beaglehole dismissed as being in the class of the mythical Phoenix or

Hippogriff), and du Fresne's find in March 1772 of a skeleton of an ass (or guanaco), and skin of a bear? All three of these species existed in South America during this period.

Distribution of Animals

The two ships sailed in relative ease across the South Pacific Ocean for weeks, before encountering new hardships. First, the men ran out of spruce beer. Then the water set aside for the horses, cows, remaining goats, pigs and sheep ran out. Fortuitously, a sudden storm saved the animals. The wind whipped up the sea which crashed onto the decks, smashing the masts and ripping the sails. They collected enough fresh rainwater to provide for the animals. Then they began to run out of hay. A choice had to be made: which of the livestock would be sacrificed so others would live? Cook gave the order to kill most of the sheep, hogs and goats, their meat to be served to the crew. Their priority was to 'keep the larger Cattle alive till we should reach some place where a fresh supply [of food] might be procured.'[40]

On 30 March 1777 they came upon a small island surrounded by a coral reef; they had reached the Cook Islands. Clerke climbed on board *Resolution* for a meeting with Cook. He was shocked to find most of the pigs, goats and sheep had been eaten. The horses and cows, forced to survive on four pounds of hay and six quarts of water every twenty-four hours, were now mere skeletons. Without immediate refreshment the animals would die. Unable to land because of a reef, they sailed to another island nearby, but this too had a reef that stopped them from getting close to the shore. Searching for a way through the bar, they observed some canoes coming towards the ships. Some islanders boarded *Resolution*. As the officers escorted them around the ship, they saw the horses and cows and panicked. Then they saw the sheep and goats and were much happier as they knew, they said, 'they were birds.'[41]

Their chief spied the ship's dogs and asked for one. While one of the gentlemen on board owned a breeding pair of dogs 'which were great nuisances in the ship, and which might have served to propagate a race of so useful an animal in this island',[42] he refused to part with them. The chief turned to one of the canoes that was laden with coconuts, plantain and a hog, offering them in trade for a dog. Cook tried offering him other articles, but he refused them all; he would only trade for a dog. Omai saw an opportunity to save some of the starving animals, including those that were reserved for him when he returned home. He had a favourite dog he had brought with him from England. He offered the dog to the chief for the plantain. The animals devoured the fresh food. However, there was not enough to sustain them for long. The following morning Omai and several of the officers took two longboats to the edge of the reef. The islanders met them in their canoes and conveyed them across the bar to the shore. While trading on the beach, Omai was delighted to see his dog happily playing on the sand, surrounded by excited and curious people. That evening they had sufficient greens to feed the animals for a few more days.

They went looking for more the next day. Coming to an uninhabited island, they were able to gather coconuts for each ship, as well as 'some grass for the cattle, and as much as they could load of leaves and branches of the young cocoa-trees, and of the tree called Wharra, [pandanus or screw pine] which being cut small, was eaten by the cattle with great greediness.[43]

On 30 April 1777 they anchored in the Tongan harbour of Rotterdam (Nomuka Island), surrounded by numerous little boats and the fragrance of tropical blossoms. The wellbeing of the animals took precedence, and within two days, the livestock were freely grazing on shore half a mile away from the sea. When the animals were brought back to the ship two weeks later, they were 'amazingly recovered; from perfect skeletons the horses and cows had grown plump, and as playful as young colts.[44]

Having exhausted Rotterdam of most of its surplus produce, Cook decided it was time to move on. They proceeded to the nearby island of Lifuka, another one of the 'Friendly Islands' (as Cook had called the Tongan Islands in 1773). There they were entertained, participated in feasts and procured more fresh supplies. It was on Lifuka that Omai received more lessons in horse riding and where Cook told him two of the horses were for him.[45] It was also on Lifuka that the son of a visiting chief tried to steal some of *Discovery*'s cats. Either Clerke was very fond of his cats, or he had a huge dislike or fear of rats. Whatever the reason, he was very upset by the theft and complained that the thief 'did not take the Rats with them.'[46] When the boy was caught, Clerke ordered him put in irons. The locals were horrified. Clerke would not release the boy unless someone returned the cats. 'Clerke was especially troubled with an infestation of rats and he needed every last one of his felines to combat them.'[47] Tensions amongst the Europeans

and the Polynesians intensified. Cook had lost his earlier lenient approach. He was now in a mood to discipline any islanders who defied him. Urged on by Omai and some of his officers, he became increasingly severe with people who stole from the ships. Cook would explode into violent rages with the minutest of provocation. The islanders were flogged, their ears cropped, people were put in irons, arms were slashed with knives and Clerke shaved the heads of anyone he caught stealing. Cook and Clerke had never meted out punishments like this previously.[48] The voyagers were no longer welcome. Resentment grew, the islanders were unsettled, and the chief wanted them off his island.

According to Edgar (the Master on *Discovery*), Clerke eventually got two of his cats back,[49] sufficient to stop the rats of *Discovery* multiplying and running amok without opposition. This enabled Clerke and Cook to continue their exploration of the Pacific Islands, distributing the livestock consistent with the instructions of George III.

On 10 June 1777 they anchored at Nuku'alofa Harbour on the island of Tongatapu (Amsterdam Island). Cook planned to stay here for at least a month, so they pitched their main tent, and landed the horses, cattle, remaining goats and sheep. Overseen by an officer, a party of marines guarded the animals. One day, a goat was seized and her shoulder bone broken. She died shortly afterwards. The theft of animals became Cook's greatest concern. To prevent further thefts, he declared his intention to leave some animals behind as gifts to the Tongan people.

Cook assembled the chiefs together and distributed the animals. They gave two rabbits, a buck and a doe, to one chief, and gave another 'a young boar, and three young sows, of the English breed. They were exceedingly desirous of them, judging, no doubt, that they would greatly improve their own breed which is rather small.'[50] To the king he gave a young English bull and a cow. Being an English breed, the bull would likely have been of the common type found in England as depicted by Bingley in 1809, such as the horned Devonshire, Herefordshire, Sussex, Northern short-horned (i.e. Durham), Lancashire or Alderney. If he was a hornless breed, he could have been Suffolk Dun, Galloway or the Northern/Yorkshire polled. However, given the limited space

The Arabian and Hunter horses, Bewick 1800: 3-5

available on *Resolution*, it was most likely to have been a small, quiet, short-horned meat breed such as the Durham. The cow's origins are unclear. She may have been English or one of the cows picked up in Cape Town.

To the king's father-in-law Cook gave a Cape Town ram and two ewes. To a chief he allotted a horse and mare. Cook had loaded the horses in Cape Town. Based on the description that Omai's horses were of a delicate breed, it is likely the horses introduced into the South Pacific by Cook were Persian or Arabian crossbreeds. Possibly of the Race horse Royalist or the Hunter Skylark variety, both of which were available in Cape Town in the 1770s.

After Cook handed over the animals, he asked Omai to explain to the new owners how rare they were in the Pacific, and that they must not kill any of them until they had increased in numbers. Conscious that the Polynesians knew little about these animals, Cook offered to have some of the islanders trained in animal husbandry. Maealiuaki, a principal chief on Tongatapu, was given the ram and ewes from the Cape, but he showed no interest in the sheep and Cook took them back. Cook had intended to give Maealiuaki a buck and two does, but seeing the man's indifference to the sheep, instead gave the goats to the king. The seamen were preparing fireworks to entertain the islanders, when two turkeys, a doe kid and a peacock were stolen from *Discovery*. Furious, Cook immediately seized three canoes that were near the ships and proclaimed he would keep them until all possessions stolen from them were returned. The stolen animals, as well as some other missing items, were duly restored.

Prior to their leaving the Tongan islands, Cook ordered the horses, bull, cow, sheep and goats be taken to a place nearer their new owners, fearing that if they were left where they were being held, once unguarded by the marines they would soon disappear. This precaution proved effective, as twenty-two years later, William Bligh, (master on *Resolution*) returned to Tonga as captain of *Bounty*. The cattle left there during Cook's last voyage had all bred, and some of the old ones were still living. Before Cook and Clerke sailed for Tahiti, the rabbits had already produced a litter of kits.

On 12 July they arrived at the Tongan island of 'Eua (Middelburg) where they received a friendly welcome, fresh water, numerous yams and a few hogs. Seeing the island had no dogs to bother the sheep, Cook gave the islanders the ram and two ewes from the Cape. On his second day on 'Eua, Cook walked to the top of the highest peak on the island, stopping to admire the view. Cook was a man rarely moved to making emotive statements. However, he wrote in his journal: 'I could not help flattering myself with the idea some future navigator may from the very same station behold these meadows stocked with cattle, the English have planted at these islands.'[51] When his servant, William Collett, went for a walk and was attacked, Cook's admiration turned to frustration. Collett's clothes were torn off him and he was left naked, with only his shoes on his feet. In retaliation, Cook confiscated two canoes and a hog. The clothes were returned in shreds, and all but one of the offenders, a young boy, had scattered. Cook returned the canoes, paid for the hog, and set his course for Tahiti.

TAHITI AND SPANISH BREEDS

It took a month to sail from the Friendly Islands to Tahiti. On 12 August they approached their first anchorage in Tahiti, Vaitepiha Bay. As the remaining livestock were disembarked, Cook learnt the Spanish had been there twice since his earlier voyage and had left behind goats, hogs, two breeds of dogs, plus one bull and a ram, 'but never a female of either of these species.'[52] The Spanish dogs had killed the ram. The hogs had interbred with the local pigs and because the islanders preferred the larger breeds of pigs, the inevitable result was 'that the Polynesian pig became extinct through interbreeding.'[53] To ensure the Tahitians could commence a breeding programme for the cattle and sheep, Cook gave them a bull, three cows, a ram and five ewes. He also left them four varieties of poultry which, given they already had fowl, were probably peacocks, geese, turkeys and ducks. Cook had planned to leave Omai's horse and mare with him at Vaitepiha Bay, but Omai decided he wanted to return to Huahine. As they prepared to sail, the last two horses were loaded onto *Resolution*.

Leaving Vaitepiha Bay, they sailed for Matavai Bay, arriving there on 24 August. Here they were welcomed by the Tahitian king — their old acquaintance, Otoo. The animals were put on shore and, to the delight and amusement of the Tahitians, Omai's horses were exercised daily. When Omai tried to ride them he kept falling off, so Cook and Clerke took to riding the horses around Matavai.[54] Cook learnt the Spanish had also called into Matavai Bay. They had left behind a large and rather wild bull which remained tied securely to a tree. Cook put three cows he had on board to the Spanish bull, then gave the king the cows, another bull and most of the remaining sheep that remained in the vessels. On observing that the goats he left there during his second voyage were now plentiful, exceedingly healthy and very tame, Cook presented the king with more animals, including 'a peacock and hen; a turkey cock and hen, one gander and three geese, a drake and four ducks. The geese and ducks began to breed before our navigators left.'[55]

Bligh later reported: 'The cows … had produced eight calves and the ewes' ten young ones. The ducks, among which they classed the geese, had greatly increased; but the turkeys and peacocks, whatever was the cause, had not bred.'[56]

The remaining animals, other than the milking goats, pets and ships' cats, were intended for Omai when he was resettled at Huahine. Cook had completed King George III's instructions to stock the Pacific Islands with livestock. Relieved of the burden of distributing livestock, he was now ready to embark on the next stage of the journey: to search for the presumed Northwest Passage connecting the Atlantic and Pacific Oceans. 'Having thus disposed of these animals, we were now, to our great satisfaction, eased of the extraordinary trouble and vexation that had attended the bringing this cargo to such a distance.'[57]

First there was the matter of resettling Omai. On 29 September, now carrying only four of Otoo's goats destined for other Pacific islands,[58] and sufficient hogs to feed themselves during the next stage of the voyage, they prepared to set sail. When the muster was called, a member of *Discovery*'s crew was missing. Alexander Mouat, (perhaps

Ghowannahe's young lover), had fallen in love with a young Tahitian girl. He attempted to desert, accompanied by the gunner's mate, twenty-three-year-old Thomas Shaw. The two didn't get far and, when returned to the ship, only received a light punishment from Clerke following the good-natured pleas from the rest of the crew.[59]

On their way to Huahine, a dog killed a young ram of the Cape Town breed. 'The loss of the ram was considered a serious misfortune as it was the only one Cook had of that breed; and of the English breed a single ram was all that remained.'[60] There is no mention of what became of the dog.

The one species of animal that was prolific on both *Resolution* and *Discovery* at this time was the rat. Cook decided to call in to the island of Mo'orea to offload some of them. Being able to anchor within yards of the land he 'made conveniences for them to go a Shore, being in hopes some would be induced to it, but I believe we got clear of very few if any.'[61] It was on Mo'orea that Cook again demonstrated a significant change in character. The day before they left a goat was stolen. It had been left grazing amongst the huts and was guarded by several islanders. Shortly after, another goat, this one big with kid, was also taken. An enraged Cook took a party of thirty-five men around the island in search of the missing goats. When the people denied knowledge of the animals' whereabouts, Cook ordered several of the houses be set alight and the destruction of ten of their largest canoes. He sent a man to the chief with a warning. Unless the goats were returned, he would destroy all their canoes. The threat worked and the goats returned, but Cook's retaliatory actions to achieve this outcome, so out of character, troubled his men.

HMS Resolution and Discovery at Morea. Royal Museums Greenwich, BHC1896, Wikimedia commons.

Omai arrives home

On 12 October 1777, two days after leaving Mo'orea, they anchored at Fare, Huahine. Several chiefs and many people, including some of Omai's relatives, greeted them. Omai was in his element. He had returned as the bountiful hero. Dressed in an English suit, he presented the High Priest with gifts of red feathers and English cloth. He talked of being welcomed by King George III, and he had brought back gifts of animals that would be highly beneficial to his people. He showed them his own animals, including the two horses, telling them of 'many other new and useful animals that had been left at Otahaite, which would speedily multiply, and furnish a sufficient number for the use of all the neighbouring islands.'[62] To the Ra'iātea people who had fled from the Bora Bora invaders to Huahine, he promised he would return to their island with his sword, horses and suit of armour and slay their enemies. Cook did not think this was such a good idea. Omai had little chance of succeeding on his own, and Cook would not interfere with local politics. He asked the Huahine chiefs to provide Omai with a small acreage of land. They gave him one and a half acres situated between the hills and the harbour, sufficient to support Omai and the two Māori boys, Tiberua and Kohaw, who were to remain as Omai's servants. Cook recompensed the chiefs with hatchets, nails and other European commodities. He put the ships' carpenters to work, building a house big enough for Omai and the boys. Other men planted a garden and created a paddock for Omai's animals.

With Omai now settled, Cook could focus on the wellbeing of his men. They put the sick on shore, away from the putrid air of the ships. Clerke and Anderson were both unwell, showing symptoms of tuberculosis. Cook was also sick and on the doctor's advice was confined to a hospital bed on shore. His health deteriorated so rapidly that the surgeons from *Resolution* and *Discovery* took turns watching over him until he was out of danger.[63] A week later Cook had recovered sufficiently to return to his ship. He was horrified to find *Resolution* infested with rats and cockroaches. The numbers of cockroaches were so phenomenal that you couldn't walk without the crunch of the insects under your feet. The damage sustained by the noxious vermin was overwhelming. Food exposed for even a few minutes was soon riddled with the vile creatures, 'who pierced it full of holes so that it resembled a honeycomb.'[64] The cockroaches destroyed stuffed bird samples and ate the labels attached to curiosities. Books, journals and charts swarmed with them. Cook ordered every crevice on the ships scraped and washed with vinegar. All beds, bedding, linen, furnishings and the men's chests were to be put on shore and fumigated. If Huahine did not have cockroaches before, they had them now. The ship was to be smoked, the portholes left open so that the rats could make their escape.

Cook accompanied Omai on his horse rides around the island. Omai was elated to be seen with the captain. He dressed in the suit of armour given to him in England, placed pistols in his holster, climbed onto his horse and went out to show his splendour to the people. Hundreds of people followed them, all yelling and cheering at the wonderful spectacle. When the crowd became too exuberant, Omai pulled out a pistol and fired it, which only succeeded in exciting the people even more.[65]

By the end of the month, Omai's house was complete, the sick had recovered and the ships were fit to sail. It was time to farewell their passenger. Along with the mare and stallion he had earlier given to Omai, Cook gave him an English boar and two English sows to accompany two sows he already owned. He also gave Omai the pregnant

by Rick Scalp. In Rickman (1781) 'Journal of Captain Cook's last voyage to the Pacific ocean in Discovery, performed in the years 1776, 1777, 1778 and 1779 illustrated with cuts and a chart showing the tracts of the ships employed in this expedition.' London. Accessed: Alexander Turnbull Library, 4 December 2018. REng RICK Journ 1781b

English poultry

The English poultry transported on *Resolution* were most likely of the common dunghill, Dorking, or Game breeds.[68] At the time of Cook's voyages there were very few of the breeds of poultry in England we know today, and they were better described as 'types' specific to a region, rather than specific breed varieties. It was not until the emergence of the first poultry shows in the 1840s that today's well-known breeds such as the Orpington, Plymouth Rock and Leghorns were developed.[69] Therefore, we can safely rely on the definitive work, published in the *Rees Cyclopedia*[70] in the early nineteenth century, to identify the breeds of English poultry that reached the South Pacific during Cook's voyages. Knowledge of these breeds is enhanced with engravings dating back to 1807 by natural history artist Sydenham Edwards.

At top, left to right: Wild cock, Wild hen, Rumpless cock, Silky cock. Below; left to right, top to bottom: Hamburgh cock, Hamburgh hen, Game cock, Game hen, Bantam cock, Bantam hen.

At top, left to right: Malay cock, Malay hen, Dorking cock. Below: Dorking hen, Frizzled cock, Frizzled hen.

goat, a cow and calf, a pair of rabbits, some sheep, cats, more poultry and a monkey, 'which the Huahine people mistook for a person.'[66] The poultry were probably of an English breed.

Twelve years later, when William Bligh returned to Huahine as captain of *Bounty*, he learnt that Omai had continued to ride his horses and, wrote Bligh, 'I observed that many of the islanders who came on board had the representation of a man on horseback tattooed on their legs.[67] Omai died thirty months after Cook left, and Tiberua and Kohaw died soon after Omai. Apparently all three died of natural causes. Of all the animals which had been left with Omai, only the mare remained alive. The monkey died when it fell out of a coconut tree, but what became of the other animals is unclear.

The Last of the Pacific Islands

Cook had now achieved two of the three orders given to him at the commencement of the voyage. Omai was safely home, and animals had been distributed throughout the Pacific Islands. Cook and Clerke were now free to go in search of the Northwest Passage. On 2 November 1777 *Resolution* and *Discovery* sailed out of the harbour having procured more than 400 hogs for the next part of the voyage. They also had on board large quantities of yams and other roots and vegetables the pigs were accustomed to eating. This would ensure they would have an ongoing source of fresh meat until more pigs could be acquired. However, they were not yet finished with the Pacific Islands.

They sailed for Ra'iātea, where they stayed for a month. While they had rid themselves of a large number of cockroaches, the rats were again prolific. Cook and Clerke moored their ships close to the shore and built a stage from the ships to the land. The rats used the stage as a bridge, thus decreasing the rats on the vessels and increasing the numbers on the island. While they were at Ra'iātea, they heard that Omai's nanny goat had died while kidding. Cook sent him two goats to replace her.

On 23 November, Alexander Mouat and Thomas Shaw again went off in a canoe, and fled to the nearby island of Bora Bora. Cook sent some marines after them and they were caught seven miles north of Bora Bora, on the island of Tupai. The men were lashed, then put in irons until they were again at sea.

Before leaving Ra'iātea, Cook gave a chief the goats he had recovered at Mo'orea, and an English boar and sow to 'improve' the island breed (which was so successful they bred the Polynesian breed out of existence). From Ra'iātea they sailed for Bora Bora. Mouat had told Cook that when he and Shaw were on this island they had seen a Spanish ram. Cook left a ewe from Cape Town at Bora Bora to breed with the ram. With no further interest in the Pacific Islands, he turned his sights towards the coast of America.

In Search of the Northwest Passage

The ships headed north and crossed the equator. On 24 December 1777 they came across an uninhabited island that Cook named Christmas Island (now Kiritimati in Kiribati). There they rested for a few days, stocking up on fresh fish and turtles. Finding no fresh water on the island, they resorted to drinking turtle blood to supplement their store of water. Needing to replenish their shrinking supplies, they resumed their course to the north. In January 1778 they approached the Hawaiian (Sandwich) Islands where they obtained an abundance of pigs and turtles. On 30 March they sailed into Nootka Sound on the coast of Vancouver Island. From here they continued their search for what many now thought was a non-existent passage between the Pacific and Atlantic oceans. *(Here we skip six months of the voyage, as none of the stories involves animals.)* On 3 October 1778 they anchored at Samgoonoodha (Unalaska Island) to repair *Resolution* and *Discovery* and to refresh themselves. They left Unalaska Island on 26 October, their destination being the Hawaiian Islands where they planned to spend the winter months, then proceed west to Kamtschatka (Kamchatka, Siberia).

HAWAIIAN (SANDWICH) ISLANDS

Towards the end of November they reached Maui, what the men saw as an island paradise with its warm weather, abundance of fresh food and beautiful women. It was in Maui that a black cat from *Discovery* fell overboard. Some natives found her, still alive, about two miles from the ship. When they returned her to Clerke, so valuable was the cat that he rewarded them with a hatchet.

They left Maui for the larger island of Hawai'i, eventually sailing into the heavily populated Karakakooa (Kealakekua) Bay on 16 January 1779 where they were greeted by over a thousand canoes.

Andrew Kippis, believed to be the first biographer of Captain James Cook, claims the principal objective that engaged Cook's attention at Hawai'i was the salting of hogs for storing at sea. He credits this to the third voyage being 'likely to be protracted a year longer than their provisions were victualled. [Cook] was under a necessity of providing for the subsistence of his crews or relinquishing the prosecution of his discoveries.'[71]

On *Resolution* and *Discovery*'s arrival, the king, chiefs and priests of Hawai'i showed Cook and his men the utmost respect, kindness and civility, including the provision of a constant supply of vegetables and small hogs. 'Then there were the small pigs, always small pigs: ceremonially correct perhaps as offering to Lono [a Hawaiian deity] but not so highly esteemed by the British, who wanted big hogs, and took pains to make their more practical preferences known to the Hawaiians.'[72]

During the two weeks *Resolution* and *Discovery* were anchored in the bay, the men consumed an enormous number of hogs and other fresh provisions. Having delivered hundreds of small pigs to Cook, the local Hawaiians' supply was running out and they 'began at length to be very inquisitive about the time in which our voyages were to take their departure.'[73] Cook explained they would need to be there a few more days to prepare the ships for the next stage of their voyage. With the supply of animals and greens considerably diminished in the local area, the king asked his people to bring more hogs and vegetables from further afield to give to the travellers.

On the day they were due to leave the bay, the king invited Cook to go to his home and see the gifts that were waiting for him. Cook and James King, his Second Lieutenant, 'were astonished at the value and magnificence of the present; for it far exceeded everything of the kind which they had seen, either at the Friendly or Society Islands.'[74] As well as other numerous gifts, laid out before them were hundreds of hogs.

Loading the unexpected bounty onto both ships, early the next day Cook and Clerke sailed out of the bay. However, two days out to sea, gales and violent waves overtook them. The following night the head of the mast nearest the bow on *Resolution*

John Webber. A View of Karakakooa [today's Kealakekua], Owhyee": site of Captain Cook's death. Wikimedia Common: http://libweb5.princeton.edu/visual_materials/maps/websites/pacific/cook3/cook-karakakoa-bay.jpg

An offering before Capt Cook, in the Sandwich Islands. Webber, call no. fr407401, Alexander Turnbull Library, Wellington

was severely damaged. Unable to continue on, Cook directed the ships to return to Karakakooa Bay so it could be repaired.

Cook's End

David Samwell, the surgeon on *Discovery*, noted that on their return to the bay on the morning of 13 February 1779 he saw nothing that suggested the Hawaiians were not pleased to see them.[75] He also reported that most of the inhabitants that were there previously had returned to their villages. On the English ships' reappearance, there were few people there to greet them. With the assistance of a few locals, they quickly set about landing *Resolution*'s damaged mast and erecting the tents on their former site. Cook and Clerke appeared to be blind to the scarcity of food their presence had created, and it is likely that their return and renewed quest for food, especially pigs, would contribute to Cook's demise.

Later that afternoon a Hawaiian worker was caught stealing some tongs from *Discovery*. He was brutally flogged and sent back to shore. Soon after, another worker was observed stealing tools from *Discovery*, but realising he had been seen, leapt off the ship into a waiting canoe. Several muskets were fired at him, but he escaped unharmed. When some of the sailors next went on shore, a number of altercations occurred between them and the Hawaiians.

The following morning Cook learnt the cutter from *Discovery* had been stolen. Accompanied by armed marines, Cook went to see the king and insisted he and his family accompany them back to *Resolution*. The intent was that the royal family would be held until the cutter was returned to them.

As they marched the king and his family to the beach, crowds gathered around them, shots were fired and the news spread amongst the people that a chief had been killed. As Cook was trying to get the king into the pinnace where his young son was already ensconced, several chiefs stepped forward and held him back. By now there were estimated to be two to three thousand people on the beach. Several began to jostle Cook; one approached with a dagger: 'Cook lifted his musket and shot him with the barrel which was loaded with small shot.'[76]

Hearing the shots, the king's son begged to be let go and scrambled out of the pinnace. The crowds began to attack the marines. Cook reloaded and fired his gun at one man, instead killing a nearby chief. According to Samwell, the marines, without waiting for Cook's orders, 'opened up a general discharge of musketry, which was instantly followed by a fire from the boats. At this, Captain Cook was heard to express his astonishment: he waved his hand to the boats, and called to them to cease firing',[77] but it was too late. When the marines fired, the Hawaiians surged forward and forced the seamen into the water, killing four of them. Their lieutenant, now wounded, managed to reach the pinnace, leaving behind Cook, who could not swim. Cook took refuge near a rock. The boats, only metres away, could not reach him. In horror, the men helplessly watched their commander's last moments.

'[Cook was] holding his left hand against the back of his head, to guard it from the stones, and carrying his musket under his other arm. An Indian was seen following him [and] gave him a blow on the back of the head … the stroke seemed to have stunned

Captain Cook: he staggered a few paces, then fell on his hand and one knee, and dropped his musket. As he was rising, and before he could recover his feet, another Indian stabbed him in the back of the neck with an iron dagger.'[78] Ironically, the dagger used was one of many traded by the Europeans for pigs. Cook fell into water that was about knee-deep. More people crowded around him, pushing his head under the water. Cook struggled and tried to drag himself onto a rock. They dragged him down into deeper water. One man sat on Cook's shoulders and beat his head with a stone while others pounded his body with clubs and stones. They hauled his limp form onto some rocks where they stuck him with their daggers. As soon as one had stabbed him, another would take the instrument out of Cook's body and stab him again. When writing this account of Cook's death, Beaglehole commented on Samwell's use of the word 'stuck', suggesting he meant 'struck'. Samwell was consistent in his use of the word 'stuck'. This is a term used by farmers to describe butchering a pig and bleeding it out. When a pig is injured, it releases a bodily chemical into the bloodstream that affects the taste of the meat. Based on Samwell's description, Cook was slaughtered and stuck like a pig; he died liked an animal.

An unwilling observer, David Samwell identified the man who gave the fatal blow — the name of the chief who killed Captain James Cook was Nooah.[79]

After Cook

While the life of Captain James Cook was over, he was just one man on this voyage of discovery. Clerke took command of the expedition and set sail for Kamtschatka, arriving there on 24 April 1779. At Kamtschatka, the men were shocked to find the local people fed their dead to the dogs. On asking about the custom they were told: 'as the deceased are thus devoured by dogs, they will ensure to themselves a pleasant carriage in sledges drawn by fine dogs in the other world.'[80]

Despite his continued ill health, Clerke undertook to complete Cook's instructions to find the North-west opening connecting the Atlantic and Pacific oceans. He too was unsuccessful and, faced with the impenetrable ice of Bering Strait, a defeated Clerke gave the order to turn for home. Bedridden, succumbing to the consumption he contracted when imprisoned at the commencement of the voyage, Clerke died on 22 August 1779.

At the beginning of October 1780, *Resolution* and *Discovery* sailed into English waters. They were under the command of American-born John Gore, the experienced seaman who had sailed on *Dolphin* with Samuel Wallis and on *Endeavour* and *Resolution* with James Cook. Despite so much achievement, so many animals distributed around the Pacific Islands, Cook's final voyage ended with little fuss.

On 28 October 1780 the *Ipswich Journal* featured an article regarding the end of Cook's final voyage on page 1. The heading reads: 'Some particulars of the late voyage around the world performed in the *Discovery* and *Resolution*.' With the focus in the article being the death of Cook and Clerke, there is little celebration of what they achieved. The final paragraph underlines the end of Cook's voyages:

'Thus the *Discovery* and *Resolution* having sailed from shore to shore, without the smallest sign of obtaining a passage, by the insurmountable obstruction of that frozen continent, the ice, the most sanguine, theoretical, or practical navigators will give up, probably for ever, all hopes of finding out a passage which would undoubtedly prove a most valuable acquisition.' The elusive Northwest Passage was discovered seventy years later.

Kamtschatka dogs [Webber, Call No fR40740, Alexander Turnbull Library]

An elegy to Captain James Cook
and the animals that sailed with him
By Anna Seward, London (1780: 9–10)[81]

To these the Hero leads his living store
And pours new wonders on th' uncultur'd shore
The silky fleece, fair fruit, and golden grain;
And future herds and harvests bless the plain.
O'er the green soil his Kids exulting play,
And sounds his clarion loud the Bird of day;
The downy Goose her ruffled bosom laves,
Trims her white wing, and wantons in the waves;
Stern moves the Bull along th' affrighted shores,
And countless nations tremble as he roars.
So when the Daughter of eternal Jove,
And Ocean's God, to bless their Athens strove,
The massy trident with gigantic force
Cleaves the firm earth — and gives the stately Horse;
He paws the ground, impatient of the rein,
Shakes his high front, and thunders o'er the plain.

Cook's portrait on a plaque outside the Executive Wing of New Zealand's Parliament Buildings - The Beehive - , Wellington. (Photo by author)

ENDNOTES

1   P. Houghton (1968). *Land from the Masthead*. London: Hodder & Stoughton: 347.

2   Anderson 1784: 414.

3   Ibid: 1249.

4   J. Rickman & D. Henry (1781). *Journal of Captain Cook's last voyage to the Pacific Ocean on Discovery, performed in the years 1776, 1777, 1778, 1779*. London: printed for E. Newbery, London: 19.

5   Ledyard, J. (1783). *A journal of Captain Cook's last voyage to the Pacific Ocean, and in quest of a north-west passage between Asia & America, performed in the Years 1776, 1777, 1778, and 1779*. Hartford: printed and sold by Nathaniel Patten: 8.

6   Holmes 1982: 20.

7   Cook in Beaglehole 1967: 1520.

8   Rickman 1781: 32.

9   G. Williams (1997). *Captain Cook's voyages: 1768–1779*. London: The Folio Society: 315.

10   Low 1892: 264.

11   Samwell in Beaglehole 1967: 991.

12   Ibid: 993.

13   Ibid: 267.

14   D. Samwell (1779). A *Narrative of the death of Captain James Cook, to which are added some particulars, concerning his life and character*. London: Hawaiian Historical Society Reprints, (No. 2): 12 February 1777.

15   Williams 1997: 321.

16   Salmond 1997: 121.

17   Anderson 1784: 430.

18   Salmond 1997: 145.

19   W. Ellis (1782). *An authentic narrative of a voyage performed by Captain Cook and Captain Clerke, in His Majesty's ships Resolution and Discovery, during the years 1776, 1777, 1778, 1779 and 1780; in search of a North-West passage between the continents of Asia and America ... Including a faithful account of all their discoveries, and the unfortunate death of Captain Cook*. (3rd ed.). Vol. 1. London: Printed for G. Robinson, J. Sewell, and J. Debrett: 26.

20   Williams 1997: 323.

21   Salmond 2003: 316–17.

22   J.C. Loudon (1835). *An Encyclopaedia of Agriculture: comprising the theory and practice ... of the animal and vegetable productions of agriculture*. Longman, Rees, Orme, Brown, Green & Longman: 1050.

23   Holmes 1982: 16.

24   Te Matangi-au-ura-nui (Salmond 1997: 127).

25   His tribal affiliation is not known.

26   Holmes 1982: 431.

27   J.R.H. Andrews (1986). *The Southern Ark: zoological discovery in New Zealand 1769–1900.* Century Hutchinson New Zealand Ltd: 34.

28   R.K. Cooper & J. Brooke (1982). 'Past and present distribution of the feral European rabbit, Oryctolagus cuniculus, on southern African offshore islands', *South African Journal of Wildlife Research,* 12: 2.

29   Anderson 1784: 432.

30   Rickman 1781: 69.

31   Ibid: 70.

32   Anderson 1784: 430.

33   Rickman 1781: 60–62.

34   Salmond 2003: 318–19.

35   A.C. Begg & N.C. Begg (1969). *James Cook and New Zealand.* Wellington: A.R. Shearer, Government Printer: 153–54.

36   Ledyard 1783: 21.

37   Salmond 2003: 316.

38   Cook & King 1785: 131.

39   Cook 1776-1779: 142

40   McNab 1914b: 22.

41   Rickman 1781: 77–78.

42   Anderson 1784: 440.

43   Rickman 1781: 82.

44   Ibid: 95.

45   Salmond 1997: 134.

46   Clerke in Beaglehole 1967: 1310.

47   McLynn 2011: 298.

48   Salmond 1997: 134.

49   Beaglehole 1967: 108

50   Ibid: 368.

51   Beaglehole 1974: 545.

52   R. McNab (1908). *Historical Records of New Zealand.* Vol. 1. Wellington: Government Printer: 30.

53   J. Newell (2010). *Trading Nature: Tahitians, Europeans, and ecological exchange.* Honolulu: University of Hawaii Press: 174–75.

54   Beaglehole 1974: 555.

55   A. Kippis (1788). *A narrative of the voyages around the world performed by Captain James Cook. With an account of his life during the previous and intervening periods.* Philadelphia: Porter & Coates: 317–18.

56   Bligh 1792: 31 October 1788.

57 J. Rickman (1790). *A Collection of Voyages Round the World, Containing a Complete Historical Account of Captain Cook's First, Second, Third and Last Voyages, in the Years 1768–1780*. London: Printed for Miller, Law & Cater: 1520.

58 Beaglehole 1974: 557.

59 A.D. Couper (2009). *Sailors and Traders: a maritime history of the Pacific Peoples*. Honolulu: University of Hawaii Press: 65.

60 Ibid: 320.

61 Beaglehole 1967: 226

62 Rickman 1790: 1590.

63 Ibid: 1592.

64 Ibid: 1593.

65 Rickman 1790: 1520.

66 Salmond 2009: 445.

67 Bligh 1792: 5 April 1789.

68 Loudon 1835: 1085.

69 John Palmer, private correspondence.

70 A. Rees (1820). *The Cyclopædia; or, Universal Dictionary of Arts, Sciences, and Literature*. Plates, Vol. 5. *Natural History*. London: Longman, Hurst, Rees, Orme and Brown: 144–46.

71 Kippis 1788: 372.

72 Sahlins 1995: 45.

73 Kippis 1788: 372.

74 Ibid: 619.

75 Samwell 1779: 13 February 1779.

76 Salmond 2003: 413.

77 Samwell 1779: 13.

78 Kippis 1788: 385

79 Samwell 1779: 16.

80 Rickman 1790: 1672.

81 A. Seward (1780). *Elegy on Captain Cook. To which is added, an Ode to the Sun*. London: J. Dodsley: 9–10.

PART FOUR

IN THE WAKE OF COOK'S ARK

Animals Cook distributed

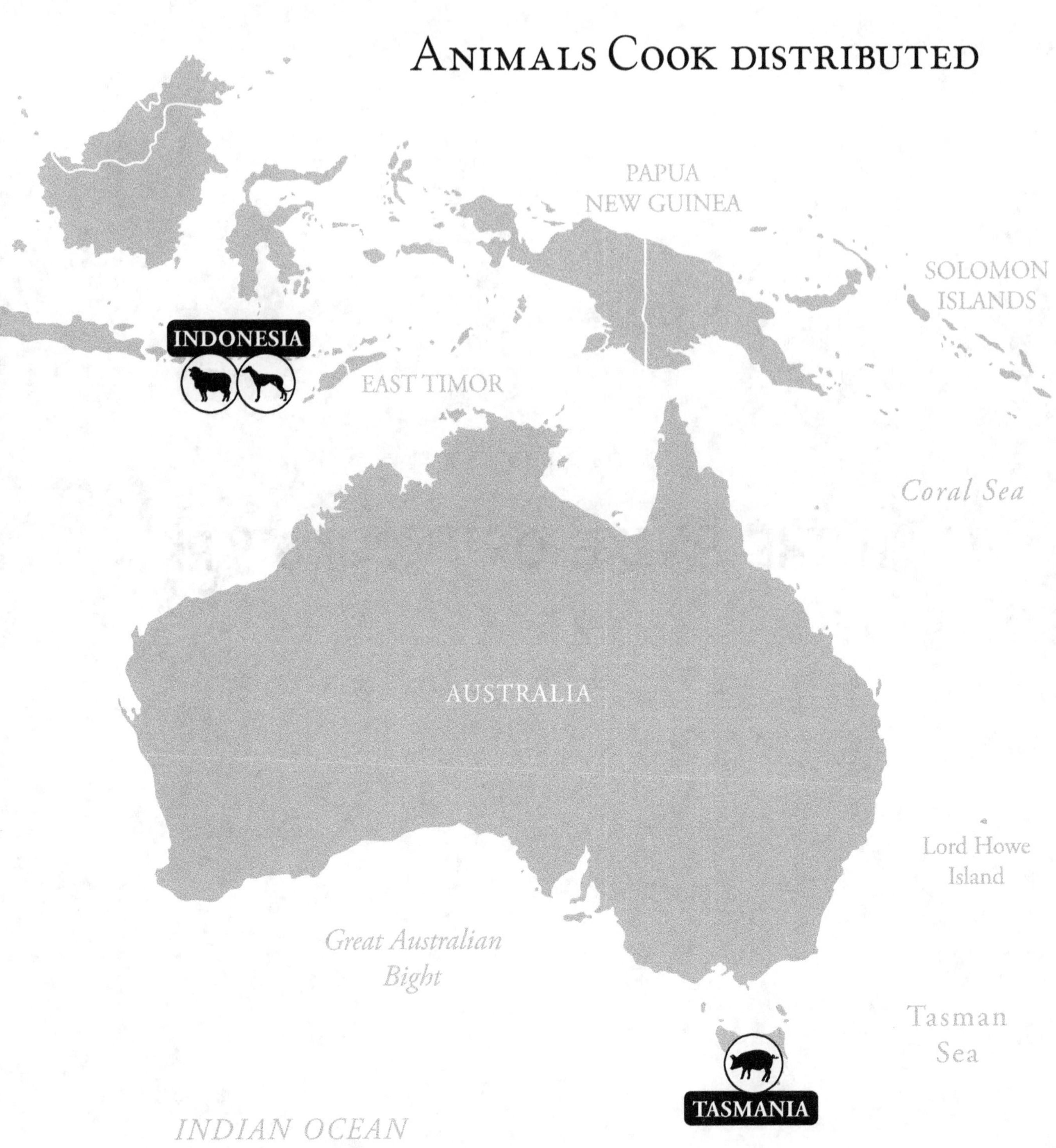

AROUND THE SOUTH PACIFIC

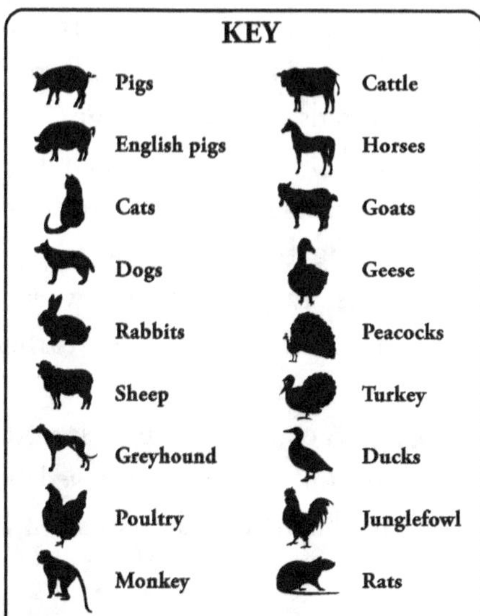

Chapter 7

THE ANIMAL LEGACY

One of the legacies from Cook's voyages to the South Pacific is the introduction of livestock. During his first circumnavigation, Cook became aware of a scarcity of animal species in the Pacific Islands, and even less in New Zealand. Faced with the reality of cannibalism practised by Māori, Cook assumed a connection between the repugnant practice and a lack of livestock. On his return to England, Cook reported his concerns to King George III. A country's need for livestock was something 'Farmer' George could relate to. It was the king's decision to introduce useful livestock into New Zealand, and it was his desire that these would be English breeds.

Given the distance and the practicalities of long sea voyages, the obvious choice of livestock were small to medium-sized animals with a high fecundity. They needed to be a proven source of food, easily transportable and able to survive in the wild. Fitting this criteria were pigs, poultry and goats. Less robust but worth trialling were sheep. Throughout the earlier parts of this book, there is considerable evidence that the pigs, goats and poultry introduced into New Zealand not only survived but thrived and are the ancestors of some of New Zealand's heritage breeds. These are Cook's legacy to all New Zealanders.

PIGS

The first pigs introduced into New Zealand during the period of Cook's voyages were the two pairs given to Māori in Doubtless Bay in December 1769 by de Surville. These probably originated from the Bashi Channel region and were likely to be a Taiwanese or Filipino breed. The native Philippine pig, no longer in existence, was black or black with a white belly.[1] The next introduction of pigs into New Zealand were two sows and a boar secreted by Furneaux into Cannibal Cove in June 1773. These were described in the various manuscripts as 'large' pigs. Throughout Cook's journals, he referred to English pigs as being large, and those purchased in the Pacific islands as small. We know that at least one of Furneaux's sows was pregnant, and at least one was black. The size and colour give us some clue as to their origins. We know that Cook acquired pigs at Madeira, Cape Verde and Cape Town, presumably as livestock to feed the men. It would have been idiotic to eat the king's gifts and replace them with a foreign breed, and Cook was not a stupid man. It is reasonably safe to assume the first pigs introduced by Furneaux were a domestic English breed. Therefore, they were most likely a common 'old-world' breed such as the Yorkshire White pig. Commonly known as the common farmer's pig, Yorkshire pigs were plain, thin, awkward animals with long legs and enormous, drooping ears. What distinguished them most from other pig breeds were the 'two wattles or dugs, not unlike the teats of a cow's udder, which hung down from their throats, one on each side.'[2] Three other pig breeds relatively common in England in the 1770s were the Herefordshire, Shropshire,[3] and the old Gloucester. The Gloucester was 'large, gaunt, long-legged, hardy, prolific, and dirty in colour.' In common with the Yorkshire breed, the Gloucester pig had a pair of wattles dangling from its jaw. At the time of Cook's voyages, all four breeds were systematically being 'improved' by the more productive, desirable and valuable Berkshire. Berkshires were a reddish colour with black spots, and had large ears hanging over their eyes. They were a short-legged, small-boned animal inclined towards being fat.[4] With one of the characteristics of the two original old English breeds being tassels hanging from their throats, it is conceivable that at least one of these breeds was introduced into New Zealand during Cook's voyages. New Zealand's kunekune pig, 'this country's only landrace breed',[5] which carries the wattle genes (DNA analysis has shown it to be 'a unique breed'),[6] may one day be traced back to a cross with the original, unimproved Yorkshire White or Gloucester pigs, both now extinct.

Another breed of pig unique to New Zealand is the Arapawa Island pig.

Kunekune_Pig_at_Hamilton_Zoo by Brian Gratwicke. https://commons.wikimedia.org/

Arapawa Island pig, by Betty Rowe (photo supplied by M. Trotter).

Captain Cooker, by Cameron Leslie

Today these pigs run feral on Arapaoa (formerly known as Arapawa) Island. This is the largest island (75 square kilometres) nearest to Ship Cove, the place from where

Cook distributed most of his livestock. During Cook's second and third voyages, released into the northern part of Queen Charlotte Sound were at least seven sows and four boars: two sows and a boar in February 1773, three sows and a boar in November 1773 and two breeding pairs in February 1777. We also know that some survived and that Māori moved them to other parts of the sound, or even further afield.

Arapawa pigs are undoubtedly a legacy from Cook and a New Zealand heritage breed. Left in isolation to evolve into a unique breed, it is probable the Arapawa pigs are remnants of the now extinct English old-world breeds. The origins of the Arapawa pig will remain a mystery until their DNA is compared with other pig strains.

New Zealand also has a feral pig known as the 'Captain Cooker'. It has been suggested that Captain Cookers, with their long snouts, razorbacks, agility and predominantly red or sandy-red colour (although some are black) are descendants of the English Tamworth pig.[7] This is unlikely as the Tamworth breed was founded in the early 1800s. It is more probable that the original Captain Cooker pigs originated from the Pacific Islands. During his second voyage Cook acquired Polynesian pigs in their hundreds and recorded giving two breeding pairs to a Māori chief on the East Coast of the North Island on 22 October 1773, and another breeding pair to the same group on 3 November 1773. Brian Hales, a farmer of exotic animals (predominantly sheep), resident of Wimbledon (near Pōrangahau) and living close to where these pigs were taken ashore, says, 'The pigs flourished in the natural environment of Southern

Hawke's Bay, spreading throughout its forest cover. They became known as the "Captain Cooker", having a long snout, and no curl in their tail. They were black, small and very thin, often referred to as razorbacks.'[8]

No longer in existence on the Pacific Islands due to crossbreeding with the introduced European breeds, it is feasible that the original Polynesian pigs' unique genetics have been preserved and run wild in the bush, not only along the lower East Coast of the North Island, but now also spread throughout the South Island.

Cook's Poultry

The first poultry introduced into New Zealand were the pair of white Siamese bantams given to Māori by de Surville in December 1769. The first introduction of poultry by Cook were geese. These were purchased at Cape Town and liberated in Dusky Sound in April 1773. Whether these birds survived and procreated is unknown. The next known introduction of poultry into New Zealand was in October 1773. Cook gave four hens and two roosters to Māori near Cape Turnagain. These were junglefowl purchased at Huahine. Two weeks later, meeting the same group of Māori near the entrance to Wellington Harbour, Cook gave them another two hens and two roosters. These were also obtained at Huahine. Shortly after, Cook released two hens and two roosters in West Bay and left an undisclosed number in Ship Cove. On their return to Queen Charlotte Sound a year later, they found evidence that at least one hen had survived.

More poultry were brought to New Zealand during Cook's final voyage. These were English species destined as exotic gifts for the Pacific Island chiefs, therefore it is unlikely that many, if any, were left in New Zealand. In all probability, the origins of New Zealand's foundation poultry were junglefowl. John Palmer, a retired New Zealand scientist who has vast knowledge of poultry origins and is arguably one of New Zealand's leading advisers on poultry breeds, says the fowl introduced into New Zealand during Cook's second voyage would most likely have been the red or common junglefowl that exist on many Pacific Islands, and which were descended from those domesticated some 5000 years ago in Asia.

Hens from China and New Hebrides. Gallus Gallus Linnaeus. Ball 1993: 125, Plate 2

Marquesan and Tahitian males. Ball 1933: 124, Plate 2

Cook's Goats

Villiers claimed gifts given to Māori in Queen Charlotte Sound on 23 May 1773 included goats. Cook asking Māori if the goats he had given them were still alive supports Villiers' claim. (Why would Cook ask Māori about goats he had hidden on Arapawa Island so they wouldn't be found?) The first goats known to be introduced into New Zealand by Cook were the breeding pair released into the bush on Arapawa Island in June 1773. Given that most of the goats purchased at Cape Town froze to death as they sailed into Antarctic waters, it is probable these goats were the common, or unimproved, Old English breed. Another possible introduction was 'Old Will', the goat who took off along the beach in November 1773. His body was never found so we cannot exclude the possibility that he survived. That some of the goats left during the second voyage lived is evident by the statement made to Cook by the young sailor (Ghowannahe's lover) from *Discovery*. During excursions with Clerke, he had seen goats in the bays of Queen Charlotte Sound. This was before Cook had given Matahouah a buck and a pregnant doe.

Whether or not goats released into New Zealand by Cook survived and are the ancestors of New Zealand's unique Arapawa goat has long been the focus of conjecture, polarisation and strong emotion.[9] The

Common English goat, Bewick 1800: 67

popular urban legend of the nineteenth and twentieth centuries was that the English goats introduced during Cook's second voyage survived and multiplied. These, therefore, were the final remnants of a breed — the Old English goat — that became extinct in the 1950s. An alternative viewpoint is that none of Cook's goats survived, and New Zealand's Arapawa Island goats are descendants of goats introduced decades later by European sealers and whalers.

In 2017, the coordinator of the New Zealand Arapawa Goat Association (the author of this book and of *No Ordinary Goat: the story of New Zealand's Arapawa Goats*) initiated a collaborative worldwide study by leading geneticists, in an attempt to determine the lineage of the Arapawa Island goats. The results released in 2018 clearly demonstrate the Arapawa goats are a unique breed that have a close connection to the indigenous South African breeds. Because the DNA study included samples from the Australian Rangeland breed and showed no close relationship to the Arapawa goats, we can confidently say the goats on Arapawa Island did not arrive in New Zealand via Australian sealers and whalers. From this, we can conclude that while the goats on the second voyage may or may not have survived, the goats purchased at Cape Town in November 1776 on Cook's final voyage, reluctantly handed over to Matahouah on 23 February 1777, are in all probability the ancestors of New Zealand's Arapawa Island goats. However, the urban legend of the Arapawa goat being a remnant of the Old English goat cannot be completely put to rest. While the scientific results demonstrate there is no genetic relationship between New Zealand's Arapawa goats and any known European breed, the scientists have been unable to compare them with DNA from the now-extinct Old English goat.

New Zealand's Heritage Breeds

Captain James Cook left England on his second voyage to the South Pacific with the intention of introducing livestock for the benefit of Māori. On several occasions he gifted animals to Māori and secreted some onto Arapawa Island and the western shores of Queen Charlotte Sound. That they survived and thrived to become biotic treasures that belong to all New Zealanders is evident. The pigs in particular became an invaluable resource to Māori when trading with the Europeans that followed in Cook's wake.

During James Cook's five anchorages in Queen Charlotte Sound, there were a number of transient Māori groups in the area: Ngāti Apa, Rangitāne, Ngāti Kuia and Ngāi Tahu. The research clearly indicates, however, that only one iwi was present during all five visits: Ngāi Tahu. On Cook's final anchorage, on 24 February 1777, as he was leaving the Sound, two chiefs — Te Matangiauuranui and Matahouah, both Ngāi Tahu and residing on Arapawa Island at that time — climbed on board *Resolution* and asked Cook for animals. Fearing for their safety, but reassured when the chiefs promised the animals would be

New Zealand Pah, Angas 1847: 78

protected and not killed, Cook reluctantly gave Te Matangiauuranui a boar and a sow, and Matahouah a pregnant doe and a buck. Left to adapt to the ecological environment of Arapawa Island over 240 years, the goats evolved into what are today's 'New Zealand Arapawa goats'. That the goats survived and thrived is supported by recent DNA results that prove, beyond any doubt, the goats on Arapawa Island are a unique phenotypic breed.

The animals were generally uncontained and able to wander freely amongst the thick bush that surrounded the small Māori settlements. Some of these animals wandered off and over many generations, in isolation and without human intervention, adapted to the ecological environment. These are New Zealand's historic heritage breeds.

The protection promised by the Ngāi Tahu chiefs could not be sustained. Invasions from North Island Māori annihilated the earlier-occupying tribes of Arapawa Island;[10] Ngāi Tahu do not have kaitiakitanga (the role of guardian and protector) over Arapawa Island. Traditional areas of interest agreed between each iwi and the Crown, based on the Treaty of Waitangi claims and signed in the Deeds of Settlement for the Marlborough area, give kaitiakitanga responsibility to Ngāti Toa Rangatira, Te Ātiawa o Te Waka-a-Māui, Rangitāne o Wairau, Ngāti Kuia and Ngāti Koata. All these iwi were present at some time in Queen Charlotte Sound during Cook's voyages. Sadly, none have accepted responsibility for the safety of Arapawa Island's pigs and goats. Despite their numbers being so small that

their existence is critically endangered, this leaves all the feral animals on the island vulnerable to the Department of Conservation's eradication programme; the intent is for Arapaoa, along with other offshore islands, to be 'predator free' by 2025.

Endnotes

1   V. Porter (1993). *Pigs: a handbook to the breeds of the world.* New York: Cornell University Press: 192.

2   Culley 1794: 173–74. London. G.G. & J. Robinson.

3   Loudon 1835: 1066.

4   Ibid: 159.

5   M. Trotter & B. McCulloch (2010). *Rare Breeds of Heritage Livestock in New Zealand.* Auckland: David Bateman Ltd: 24.

6   Allen, Matisoo-Smith & Horsburgh 2001: 4–5.

7   According to G.M. Thomson (1922). *The Naturalisation of Animals and Plants in New Zealand.* Cambridge: Cambridge University Press.

8   Personal communication.

9   B. Rowe (1988). *Arapawa: once upon an island.* Auckland: The Halcyon Press.

10   Elvy 1997.

REFERENCES

Allan, J., Ensor, R., Le Fevre, P. (2004). *Thomas Luny and Cook's Resolution.* The Mariner's Mirror, 90:1, 85–102.

Allen, M. S., Matisoo-Smith, E., Horsburgh, A. (2001). *Pacific 'Babes': issues in the origins and dispersal of Pacific pigs and the potential of mitochondrial DNA analysis.* International Journal of Osteoarchaeology, 11: 4–13.

Anderson, G.W. & Rouse, W.H.D. (Ed.). (1906). *Captain Cook's Second Voyage.* London: Blackie & Son Ltd.

Anderson, G.W. (1784). *A new, authentic, and complete collection of voyages round the world, undertaken and performed by royal authority: containing an authentic, entertaining, full, and complete history of Captain Cook's first, second, third and last voyages, undertaken by order of his present Majesty, for making discoveries in geography, navigation, astronomy, &c. in the southern and northern hemispheres &c.* London. Printed for Alex Hogg.

Andrews, J.R.H. (1986). *The Southern Ark: zoological discovery in New Zealand 1769–1900.* Century Hutchinson New Zealand Ltd.

Angas, G.F. (1847). *Savage life and scenes in Australia and New Zealand.* Vol. 1. London. Smith, Elder & Co.

Appleton, M. (1958). *They Came to New Zealand: an account of New Zealand from the earliest times up to the middle of the nineteenth century.* London: Methuen & Co. Ltd.

Aughton, P. (1999). *Endeavour: the story of Captain Cook's first great epic voyage.* Great Britain: The Windrush Press.

Ball, S.C. (1933). *Jungle Fowls from Pacific Islands.* Bernice P. Bishop Museum, Bulletin 108. Honolulu, Hawaii.

Banks, J. & Hooker, J.D. (Ed.). (1896). *Journal of the Right Hon. Sir Joseph Banks during Captain Cook's first voyage in H.M.S. Endeavour in 1768–71 to Terra del Fuego, Otahite, New Zealand, Australia, the Dutch East Indies, etc.* London: MacMillan & Co.

Banks, J. & Lysaght, A.M. (Ed.). (1980). *The Journal of Joseph Banks in the* Endeavour/ *with a commentary from A.M. Lysaght.* Vol. 2. Adelaide: Genesis Publications Ltd.

Bayly, W. (1772–1774). *Manuscript private journal kept by Will Bayly, astronomer to the second voyage of Captain Cook* 1772–1775. Wellington: Alexander Turnbull Library, National Archives. Ref: fMS-015.

Beaglehole, J.C. (1955). *The Life of Captain James Cook: The voyage of the* Endeavour, *1768–1771.* Cambridge University Press.

Beaglehole, J.C. (1974). *The Life of Captain James Cook.* London: Adam & Charles Black.

Beaglehole, J.C. (Ed.). (1961). *The Journals of Captain James Cook on his Voyages of Discovery. Vol. 2: The voyage of* Resolution *and* Adventure *1772–1775.* London: Routledge Francis Taylor & Group.

Beaglehole, J.C. (Ed.). (1962). *The Endeavour Journal of Joseph Banks 1768–1771.* (Vols. 1 & 2). Australia: Angus and Robertson.

Beaglehole, J. C. (Ed.). (1967). *The Journals of Captain James Cook on his voyages of discovery. The voyage of Resolution and Discovery, 1776-1780.* Parts 1 & 2. London: Cambridge University Press. Published for the Hakluyt Society.Begg, A.C. & Begg, N.C. (1969). *James Cook and New Zealand.* Wellington: A.R. Shearer, Government Printer.

Besant, W. (1894). *Captain Cook.* London: Macmillan & Co.

Best, E. (1918). *The Discovery & Re-Discovery of Wellington Harbour.* Wellington: Government Printing Office.

Beulah H.G. & Hancock, E.G. (2018). 'The "Lost" Types of Carabus Pallens Fabricius, 1775 (Coleoptera: Carabidae: Lebiinae) from the Banks and Hunter Collections: Lectotype Designation, Redescription, and Distribution', *The Coleopterists Bulletin* 72: 4, pp. 845–57.

Bewick, T. (1797). *History of British Birds: the figures engraved on wood.* Vol. 1. Newcastle, London.

Bewick, T. (1800). *A General History of Quadrupeds: the figures engraved on wood by T. Bewick.* (4th ed.). London, Newcastle Upon Tyne.

Bingley, W. & Howitt, S. (1809). *Memoirs of British quadrupeds illustrative principally of their habits of life, instincts, sagacity, and uses to mankind, arranged according to the system of Linnaeus. With engravings from original drawings.* London.

Bligh, W. (1792). *A voyage to the south sea, undertaken by command of his majesty for the purpose of conveying the bread-fruit tree to the West Indies, in his Majesty's ship the* Bounty, *commanded by Lieutenant William Bligh.* Printed for George Nicol, Bookseller to his Majesty, Pall-Mall. London.

Bloomfield, R. (2013) *Wake of the* Endeavour: *New Revised Edition.* Amazon Kindle Books.

Bootie, J. (1768–1771). *A journal of the proceedings of his Majesty's Bark* Endeavour. *Commencing from 27th May 1768 to the 24th Nov 1769.* Ref. 51/4546. Sydney: Mitchell Library Museum.

Boswell, J. (1822). *The life of Samuel Johnson, L.L.D: Comprehending an account of his studies and numerous works in chronological order, a series of his epistolary correspondence and conversations with many eminent persons, and various original pieces of his composition, never before published ...* In two volumes. London.

Briscoe, P. (1771). *A journal of His Majesties Bark* Endeavour *by God's permission bound to the South Seas, Lieutenant James Cook, Commander, 27th May 1768–14 May 1770.* SAFE/DLMS 96. State Library of New South Wales Collection.

Cameron, I. (1987). *Lost Paradise: the exploration of the Pacific.* London: Century.

Catton, C. (1788). *Animals, drawn from nature and engraved in aqua-tinta.* London: I & J Taylor.

Colenso, W. (1877, 8 October). *Notes, chiefly historical, on the ancient Dog of the New Zealanders.* Read before the Hawke's Bay Philosophical Institute. Christchurch: Kiwi Publishers, Retrieved: 2018 (NZ Electronic Text Collection: http://nzetc.victoria.ac.nz/ tm/scholarly/tei-NZETC).

Coleridge, S.T. (1866). *The Rime of the Ancient Mariner. Illustrated.* London: D. Appleton & Co.

Cook, J. & Furneaux, T. (1777). *A Voyage towards the South Pole and round the World: performed in His Majesty's ships the* Resolution *and* Adventure, *in the Years 1772, 1773, 1774 and 1775.* Vol. 1. London: Printed for W. Strahan and T. Cadell.

Cook, J. & King, J. (1785). *A voyage to the Pacific Ocean for making discoveries in the northern hemisphere: performed under the direction of Captains Cook, Clerke, and Gore, in the years 1776, 1777, 1778, 1779, 1780.* In three volumes. London: Published by order of the Lords Commissioners of the Admiralty.

Cook, J. (1776–1779). *Journal of H.M.S. Resolution 1776–1779 – Vol. 1 – Cook.* Wellington: Alexander Turnbull Library in the National Archives.

Cook, J., Forster, G., Smith, W. (1846). *The voyages of Captain James Cook: illustrated with maps and numerous engravings on wood: with an appendix, giving an account of the present condition of the South Sea Islands, &c.* In 2 vols. London: W. Smith.

Cook, J., Hawkesworth, J., Banks, J., Clerke, C., Gore, J. (1821). *The three voyages of Captain James Cook round the world.* 'Complete in seven volumes. Vol. III. being the first of the second voyage.' London: Printed for Longman, Hurst, Rees, Orme, and Brown.

Cook, J., King, J., Rollinson, W. (1796). *A voyage to the Pacific Ocean for making discoveries in the northern hemisphere: performed under the direction of Captains Cook, Clerke, and Gore, in the years 1776, 1777, 1778, 1779, 1780.* Vol. 3. New York. Printed by Tiebout and O'Brien, for Benjamin Gomez.

Cooper, R.K. & Brooke, J. (1982). 'Past and present distribution of the feral European rabbit, Oryctolagus cuniculus, on southern African offshore islands', *South African Journal of Wildlife Research*, 12: 2.

Couper, A.D. (2009). *Sailors and Traders: a maritime history of the Pacific Peoples.* Honolulu: University of Hawai'i Press.

Cowan, J. (1935). *A Trader in Cannibal Land: the life and adventures of Captain Tapsell.* Wellington: A.H. & A.W. Reed.

Craik, G.L. (1830). *The New Zealanders.* London: William Clowes.

Crozet, J.M. (1891). *Crozet's voyage to Tasmania, New Zealand and the Ladrone Islands and the Philippines in the years 1771–1772.* Translated by A. Rochon. Cambridge: Cambridge University Press.

Culley, G. (1794). *Observations on Live Stock: Containing hints for choosing and improving the best breeds of the most useful kinds of domestic animals. 173–174.* London. G.G. & J. Robinson.

Cunningham, D.M. & Moors, P.J. (1996). *Guide to the Identification and Collection of New Zealand Rodents.* (3rd ed.). Wellington: Department of Conservation.

Davis, C.O. (1876). *The Life and Times of Patuone, the Celebrated Ngapuhi Chief.* J.H. Field, Albert Street, Auckland: Steam Printing Office.

Day, M. (2002). *Mrs Cook: the real and imagined life of the Captain's wife.* Australia: Allen & Unwin.

Diong, C. H. (1982). *Population biology and management of the feral pig.* A dissertation submitted to the graduate division of the University of Hawaii in partial fulfilment of the requirements for the degree of Doctor of Philosophy in Zoology.

Druett, J. (2012). *Tupaia: the remarkable story of Captain Cook's Polynesian navigator.* Auckland: Random House.

Dugard, M. (2001). *Farther Than Any Man. the rise and fall of Captain James Cook.* Australia: Allen & Unwin.

Dunmore, J. (1969). *The Fateful Voyage of the* St Jean Baptiste: *a true account of M. de Surville's expedition to New Zealand & the unknown South Seas in the Years 1769–70.* Christchurch: Pegasus Press.

Dunmore, J. (2006). *Mrs Cook's Book of Recipes for Mariners in Distant Seas.* Sydney: Australian National Maritime Museum.

Edwards, G. (1858). *Gleanings of natural history, exhibiting figures of quadrupeds, birds, insects, plants etc. with … descriptions of seventy different subjects, designed, engraved and coloured after nature, on fifty copper-plate prints.* London: Printed for the author, at the Royal College of Physicians, in Warwick Lane.

Ellis, W. (1782). *An authentic narrative of a voyage performed by Captain Cook and Captain Clerke, in His Majesty's ships* Resolution *and* Discovery, *during the years 1776, 1777, 1778, 1779 and 1780; in search of a North-West passage between the continents of Asia and America ... Including a faithful account of all their discoveries, and the unfortunate death of Captain Cook.* (3rd ed.). Vol. 1. London: Printed for G. Robinson, J. Sewell, and J. Debrett.

Elvy, W.J. (1997). Kei puta te Wairau : a history of Marlborough in Māori times. Christchurch. Whitcombe & Tombs.

Erskine, N. *Cook relics — real and imagined.* Retrieved May 2018. Sydney: Australian National Maritime Museum. (http://www.nla.gov.au/events/cooks-treasures/papers/Nigel-Erskine-Cook-relics-real-and-imagined.)

Forster, G. (1777). *A voyage round the world, in His Britannic Majesty's sloop* Resolution, *commanded by Capt. James Cook, during the years 1772, 3, 4 and 5.* Digital archives and Pacific cultures. Accessed via http://pacific.obdurodon.org/ForsterGeorgComplete.html

Forster, G. (1777a). *A voyage round the world, in His Britannic Majesty's sloop* Resolution, *commanded by Capt. James Cook, during the years 1772, 3, 4 and 5.* Vol. 1. London.

Forster, G. (1777b). *A voyage round the world, in His Britannic Majesty's sloop* Resolution, *commanded by Capt. James Cook, during the years 1772, 3, 4 and 5.* Vol. 2. London.

Forster, J.R. (1778). *Observations made during a voyage round the world, on physical geography, natural history, and ethic philosophy* ... London: Robinson.

Hoare, M.E. (Ed.). (1982). *The* Resolution *Journal of Johann Reinhold Forster, 1772–1775.* (Vols 1-4). London. The Hakluyt Society.

Holmes, C. (1982). *Captain Cook's Final Voyage: the journal of Midshipman George Gilbert.* London: Caliban Books.

Holmes, E. (2017). 'Joseph Banks, botanist and patron, and: not recorded: Dorlton and Richmond, servants, and: not recorded: Girl', *Southern Review*, 53: 4, pp. 478–82. Project MUSE, muse.jhu.edu/article/663673.

Hooper, B. (1975). *With Captain James Cook in the Antarctic and Pacific: the private journal of James Burney, second lieutenant of the* Adventure *on Cook's second voyage, 1772–1773.* Canberra: National Library of Australia.

Hough, R. (1994). *Captain James Cook: a biography.* London: Hodder & Stoughton.

Houghton, P. (1968). *Land from the Masthead.* London: Hodder & Stoughton.

Huang, Y.F., Shi, X.W., Zhang, Y.P. (1999 Dec.). 'Mitochondrial genetic variation in Chinese pigs and wild boars', *Biochem Genet.* 37: 11–12, pp. 335–43.

Hunt, R. (2010). 'Joseph Banks', *New Zealand Geographic*, 101: Jan–Feb.

Kippis, A. (1788). *A narrative of the voyages around the world performed by Captain James Cook. With an account of his life during the previous and intervening periods.* Philadelphia: Porter & Coates.

Ledyard, J. (1783). *A journal of Captain Cook's last voyage to the Pacific Ocean, and in quest of a north-west passage between Asia & America, performed in the Years 1776, 1777, 1778, and 1779.* Hartford: printed and sold by Nathaniel Patten.

Loudon, J.C. (1835). *An Encyclopaedia of Agriculture: comprising the theory and practice … of the animal and vegetable productions of agriculture.* Longman, Rees, Orme, Brown, Green & Longman.

Low, C.R. (1892). *Captain Cook's three voyages round the world. With a sketch of his life.* London: George Routledge & Sons, Ltd.

Macarthur, A. (1997). *His Majesty's Bark* Endeavour: *the story of the ship and her people.* Australia: Angus & Robertson.

Mackie, E.W. (1985). *William Hunter and Captain Cook: the 18th Century ethnographical collection in the Hunterian Museum.* Glasgow.

Marra, J. (1775). *Journal of the* Resolution's *voyage: in 1772, 1773, 1774, and 1775. On* Discovery *to the southern hemisphere. Also a journal of the* Adventure's *voyage, in the years 1772, 1773, and 1774. … Illustrated with a chart, … and other cuts.* London: Printed for F. Newbery.

McLynn, F. (2011). *Captain Cook: master of the seas.* London: Yale University Press.

McNab, R. (1908). *Historical Records of New Zealand.* Vol. 1. Wellington: Government Printer.

McNab, R. (1909). *Murihiku: a history of the South Island of New Zealand and the Islands adjacent and lying to the South, from 1642 to 1835.* Wellington: Whitcombe & Tombs Ltd.

McNab, R. (1914a). *From Tasman to Marsden: a history of northern New Zealand from 1642 to 1818.* Dunedin: J. Wilkie & Co., Ltd.

McNab, R. (1914b). *Historical records of New Zealand.* Vol. 2. Wellington: Government Printer.

Mitchell, H. & Mitchell, M.J. (2004). *Te Tau Ihu o te Waka: a history of Māori of Nelson and Marlborough.* Vol. 1. Wellington: Huia Publishers.

Molyneux, R. (1768–1770). *A journal of the proceedings of His Majesty's Bark* Endeavour; *Log Transcript.* PRO Adm 51/4546/152. Sydney: Mitchell Library.

Montague, E. W. (1773), Published in the Sentimental & Masonic Magazine for July 1792, Dublin

Moore, W. (2015). *The Waterfowl Species of Southern Africa.* Windhoek, Namibia. (Accessed via www.gunsonpegs.com/the-sportsman/part-1-the-waterfowl-species-of-southern-africa).

Moran, M. (2003). *Beyond the Coral Sea: travels in the old empires of the South West Pacific.* London: Harper Collins Publishers.

Mundle, R. (2013). *Captain James Cook.* Australia: Harper Collins Publishers.

Newell, J. (2010). *Trading Nature: Tahitians, Europeans, and ecological exchange.* Honolulu: University of Hawaii Press.

O'Brian, P. (1987). *Joseph Banks: a life.* Chicago: University of Chicago Press.

Parkinson, S. & Kenrick, W. (1773). *A journal of a voyage to the South Seas in his Majesty's ship, the* Endeavour. *Faithfully transcribed from the papers of the late Sydney Parkinson. Draughtsman to Joseph Banks, Esq., on his late expedition with Dr. Solander, round the world.* London: Printed for Stanfield Parkinson.

Pennant, T. & Banks, J. (1767). *Correspondence between Thomas Pennant (22 letters) and Joseph Banks (3 Letters).* Retrieved May 1, 2018. (books.google.co.nz/books/about/).

Pennant, T. (1771). *Synopsis of Quadrupeds.* London: Chester & Monk.

Pennant, T. (1773). *History of Quadrupeds.* (Vols I & 2). London: B. & J. White.

Pickersgill, R. (1772–1773). *Journal of Richard Pickersgill, Third Lieutenant on the Resolution, Captain James Cook.* University of Cambridge University Library.

Porter, V. (1993). *Pigs: a handbook to the breeds of the world.* New York: Cornell University Press.

Rees, A. (1820). *The Cyclopædia; or, Universal Dictionary of Arts, Sciences, and Literature.* Plates, Vol. 5. *Natural History.* London: Longman, Hurst, Rees, Orme and Brown.

Reed, A.W. & Clark, R. (1956). *How the white men came to New Zealand.* A.H. & A.W. Reed, Wellington.

Rhys, E. (1906). *Captain Cook's Voyages of Discovery.* London: J.M. Dent & Sons Ltd.

Richmond, M.S., Satterfield, G.H., Grinnells, C.D., Dann, W.J. (1940). 'Ascorbic acid content of goat's milk and blood: influence of ascorbic acid injection and diet', *The Journal of Nutrition*, 20: 2, pp. 99–108.

Rickman, J. & Henry, D. (1781). *Journal of Captain Cook's last voyage to the Pacific Ocean on* Discovery, *performed in the years 1776, 1777, 1778, 1779.* London: printed for E. Newbery, London.

Rickman, J. (1790). *A Collection of Voyages Round the World, Containing a Complete Historical Account of Captain Cook's First, Second, Third and Last Voyages, in the Years 1768–1780.* London: Printed for Miller, Law & Cater.

Roberts, J. (1771). *A journal of His Majesty's bark* Endeavour *round the world, Lieut. James Cook, Commander, 27th May 1768', 27 May – 14 May 1770, with annotations.* Mitchell Library, Australia.

Robertson, G. & Carrington, H. (1948). *The discovery of Tahiti. A journal of the second voyage of H.M.S.* Dolphin *round the world, under the command of Captain Wallis, R.N. in the years 1766, 1767 and 1768.* London: The Hakluyt Society.

Robson, J. (2000). *Captain Cook's World: maps of the life and voyages of James Cook R.N.* Auckland: Random House.

Robson, J. (2009). *Cook's Log.* https://captaincooksociety.com/.

Rowe, B. (1988). *Arapawa: once upon an island.* Auckland: The Halcyon Press.

Sahlins, M. (1995). *How 'Natives' think: about Captain Cook, for example.* Chicago: University of Chicago Press.

Salmond, A. (1991). *Two Worlds: first meetings between Māori and Europeans 1642–1772.* Honolulu: University of Hawaii Press.

Salmond, A. (1997). *Between Worlds: early exchanges between Māori and Europeans 1773–1815.* Auckland: Viking Penguin Books.

Salmond, A. (2003). *The Trial of the Cannibal Dog: Captain Cook in the South Seas.* London: Allen Lane for the Penguin Press.

Salmond, A. (2009). *Aphrodite's Island: the European discovery of Tahiti.* Auckland: Viking Penguin.

Samwell, D. (1779). *A Narrative of the death of Captain James Cook, to which are added some particulars, concerning his life and character.* London: Hawaiian Historical Society Reprints, (No. 2).

Seward, A. (1780). *'Elegy on Captain Cook'. To which is added, an Ode to the Sun.* London: J. Dodsley.

Sherrin, R., & Wallace, J. (1890). *Early history of New Zealand Brett's historical series, from earliest times to 1840, by R.A.A. Sherrin. From 1840 to 1845, by J. H. Wallace.* In T.W. Leys (Ed.). Auckland: H Brett.

Smith, C.H. (1840). *The Natural History of Dogs: canidae or genus canis of authors; including also the genera hyaena and proteles.* Vol. 2. Edinburgh.

Smith, W. (1842). *The Voyages of Captain James Cook round the world*, Vol. 1. London. https://australianmuseum.net.au/image/endeavour-in-tahiti-1769.

Sparrman, A. (1785). *A Voyage to the Cape of Good Hope: towards the Antarctic polar circle, and round the world: but chiefly into the country of the Hottentots and Caffres, from the year 1772 to 1776.* Translated from the Swedish original. (Vols 1 & 2). London: G.G.J. & J. Robinson.

Sparrman, A. (1953). *A Voyage Round the World with Captain James Cook in H.M.S. Resolution.* Translated by Huldine Beamish & Averil Mackenzie-Grieve. London: Robert Hale Ltd.

Stevens, R.W. (1858). *On the Stowage of Ships and their Cargoes.* London: Stevens, Plymouth. Longmans.

Sutherland, A. (2016). *No Ordinary Goat: the story of New Zealand's Arapawa Goats.* Wellington: NZ Arapawa Goat Association.

Thomson, G.M. (1921). *Wildlife in New Zealand. Part I.—Mammalia.* Wellington: Government Printer.

Thomson, G.M. (1922). *The Naturalisation of Animals and Plants in New Zealand.* Cambridge: Cambridge University Press.

Trotter, M. & McCulloch, B. (2010). *Rare

Breeds of Heritage Livestock in New Zealand. Auckland: David Bateman Ltd.

Turner, G. (1861). *Nineteen Years in Polynesia: missionary life, travels and researches in the islands of the Pacific.* Paternoster Row, London: John Snow.

Vance, W. (1976). *Bush, bullocks, and boulders.* The Alford Forest Bushside Springburn District Centenary Committee.

Villiers, A. (1967). *Captain Cook, the seamen's seaman.* UK. London: Hodder & Stoughton.

Wadsworth, T. (2015). *The spatial distribution of pā in Tōtaranui/Queen Charlotte Sound, New Zealand.* A thesis submitted for the degree of Master of Arts, University of Otago, Dunedin, New Zealand.

Williams, G. (1997). *Captain Cook's voyages: 1768–1779.* London: The Folio Society.

Wodzicki, K.A. (1950). *Introduced mammals of New Zealand. An ecological and economic survey.* Wellington. Department of Scientific & Industrial Research Bulletin No. 98.

V
Vaitepiha Bay (Oaitepeha) 80, 136
Vanuatu *see* New Hebrides
Venus, transit of 2, 11, 19, 21

W
Waihou River 31
Waikawa 27, 88, 109
Wales, William 61, 66, 95
Wallis, Samuel 2, 4, 10, 16, 32, 51, 55, 59,
    80, 148, 169
Webber, John 17, 63, 81–83, 117, 126,
    130, 145–146, 149
Weir, Alexander 9
Wellington Harbour
    (Te Whanganui-a-Tara) 89, 92, 157,
    164
West Bay 95, 108, 157
Whitehouse, John 66
Wilkinson, Francis 2
Woodhouse, Thomas 97
wort 23, 100

Y
Young, Nicholas 23, 47
Young Nick's Head
    (Te Ūpoko-o-te-kurī-a-Paoa) 23